AF690874

I STAND ON MY BRIEFS

Pro Se Legal Warfare

Gregory Stenstrom

Four Dolphins Publishing
Glen Mills, Pennsylvania

I Stand on My Briefs
Pro Se Legal Warfare (PSLW)
A Strategic Litigation Framework for Pro Se and Adversarial Proceedings

Copyright © 2025-2026 by Gregory Stenstrom
All rights reserved.

No part of this publication may be reproduced, distributed, or transmitted in any form or by any means, including photocopying, recording, or other electronic or mechanical methods, without the prior written permission of the publisher, except in the case of brief quotations used in reviews or other uses permitted by copyright law.

Library of Congress Control Number: 2026909009

Subject Categories: Law / Civil Procedure / Litigation Strategy / Pro Se Practice

ISBN: 979-8-218-90141-7 (Hardcover)

First Edition
First published May 13, 2026 by Four Dolphins Publishing
Glen Mills, Pennsylvania

Printed in the United States of America

Author Disclaimer: This work describes litigation patterns and presents doctrinal responses grounded in procedural law and record preservation. It is provided for educational and informational purposes only and does not constitute legal advice or create an attorney–client relationship. Readers are solely responsible for their use and application of the material.

Opening Prayer

"He has shown you, O man, what is good;
And what does the Lord require of you
But to do justice, to love mercy,
And to walk humbly with your God?" – Micah 6:8

In the name of Jesus Christ, the Righteous Judge and our Advocate, we lift this work and all who read it into Your light.

We pray for the honest judge,
who remembers that the robe is not a crown,
but a trust to apply law with courage and integrity.

We pray for the fearless litigant,
who enters the arena alone, armed only with truth,
and refuses to be broken by corruption or delay.

We pray for the clerk and staff member,
who preserves the record faithfully,
knowing that without a true record there can be no justice.

We pray for the officer of the court and the law,
who guards the oath and protects the people,
not the powerful.

And we pray for every citizen who still believes that courts can be noble,

and that each act of honesty, each demand for accountability,
restores them to what they were meant to be.

May this book be a light to those who fight alone,
a reminder to those who serve within the system,
and a testimony to all that justice, tempered with mercy,
is Your design for a civilized people.

This book is for them, and for You.

All glory to God for his divine signal.

In Jesus' name. Amen.

Acknowledgments

All things are brought to us by the grace of God and the choices we make. All praise, glory and honor to God.

I would like to thank my wife and inspiration, Lilliana, who loves the United States of America as much as I do, for her love and unwavering support. Her journey to citizenship, to make a better life under the blanket of our Constitution and laws, is the story of our nation.

My mother, father, brothers, and family have been, and remain, my forever guides to my true north.

My sons, daughter, and grandchildren will live in the world we leave to them and they, most of all, are why I persevere.

I have many friends, and as with all friendships, some change your life. A small cadre of patriots and Godly people I am blessed to be part of are the **Deep Divers**. Of all the people in my life besides my family, they helped most in renewing my faith in God - and in people. They are, Paul Rumley and Scott Thomas, who restored me back to the Roman Catholic faith, and a deep love of Jesus and Mary that I remembered as a young child. Carris and Erik Kocher, whose embodiment of the Holy Spirit is an example for us all. Joy Schwartz, John Proctor Child, Laura Lewis, Nick

Manganaro, Robert Mancini, Kathy Buckley, Kathy McGuigan, and Leah Hoopes—it has been a privilege to earn your friendship and respect, and an honor to serve with you in Christ.

To Renee Mazer and John Cellucci, my close friends and legal confidantes, you are among the only licensed attorneys I know who are unwaveringly righteous.

To the handful of my friends who I allow myself to be vulnerable with—who see the best and very worst of me and remain steadfast: Phil Barnabei, Kay Romasko, Todd Berringer, and Michael Clinger – thank you.

Special mention goes to my Naval Academy '83 classmate, fellow warrior and patriot, Dr. Timothy Shindelar, Colonel (USMC, Retired), who courageously (and relentlessly) is willing to fight and slug it out with me intellectually, and honed many of the strategies and tactics herein. History should remember you as a true American hero, as I do.

Maybe most importantly, I must thank the unending line of weak or corrupt clerks, lawyers, and judges who have been the grist and whetstones that have sharpened my litigative tools. I pray regularly for your deliverance from hell.

Last, but not least, to my business partner, Co-Founder of Patriot.Online and Patriot Internet Corporation, and spiritual brother—Scott Randall—my daily sanity check lifeline and fellow traveler.

— Gregory Stenstrom
October 22, 2025

Table of Contents

Why Scripture Frames This Book

(A Note on First Principles, Law, and the Divine Compass That Guides Them)

The use of Old Testament verses to open each chapter—and New Testament verses to close them—is deliberate. It serves two purposes, neither ornamental nor rhetorical.

First, it reflects my own warrior ethos and true north. I draw strength from the belief that justice comes from a higher law—one not written by men, but revealed to them. That belief steadied me in dark times, hostile courts, and long nights when endurance mattered more than victory. Scripture is not a performance. It is my anchor.

Second, and more importantly for the reader, Scripture is the rootstock of every rule-based system of law in Western Civilization—including the United States.
Whether or not one is Christian, Jewish, or secular, this is a historical and legal fact:

The Old Testament is the foundation of natural law, moral philosophy, justice, rights, due process, and covenantal obligation.

The New Testament shaped the ethics that informed St. Thomas Aquinas' "*Summa Theologiae*," the Magna Carta, English common law, Blackstone's "*Commentaries on the Laws of England*," the Federalist Papers, and ultimately the U.S. Constitution.

You cannot understand Western law—or its conception of justice—without understanding its source.
You may reject the theology, but you cannot deny the lineage.

The Bible is not merely a religious text. It is the first legal textbook, the first body of written case law, the first articulation of equal justice, judicial restraint, evidentiary standards, due process, mercy, and the idea that no ruler stands above the law.

Every major legal scholar—from Aquinas and Blackstone to Adams and Madison—regarded Biblical law as the bedrock of civil society. The Constitution did not arise from a vacuum; it is the latest expression of a 3,000-year conversation about justice that began with Moses.

Unless otherwise noted, Scripture quotations and numbering conventions primarily follow the Douay-Rheims tradition, with occasional Septuagint and Hebrew textual parallels where doctrinally or historically appropriate.

The Old Testament verses placed at the start of each chapter represent the origin of law: justice, order, truth, obligation, restraint.

The New Testament verses at each chapter's end represent the fulfillment of law: equity, mercy, conscience, and disciplined action.

This structure is not a sermon.
It is the architecture of law itself.

It is also a reminder—to every reader, believer or otherwise—that law unmoored from moral compass becomes mere power. Courts that forget their roots in justice quickly become instruments of control. Lawyers who forget that truth precedes argument drift into sophistry. Judges who forget that their oath rests upon something higher than their own preferences inevitably fall into arrogance.

You cannot practice law, fight corruption, or survive in a courtroom without a compass.
Scripture is mine—and it is the compass from which Western law itself was built.

If you do not share that faith, the doctrines of this book still stand—they require no theology to function. But the moral and philosophical framework behind them comes from the same foundation that gave us the right to speak, to file, to petition, to confront accusers, to demand due process, and to restrain government power.

Our legal tradition holds that rights are inherent—not granted by the State, but recognized as preexisting the State.

The entire Anglo-American legal tradition is built on natural law—the recognition that law derives from enduring moral principles, not from the mere will of governments.

Jesus—whether seen as the Son of God, a prophet, or a historical teacher—was a legal teacher. His lifetime revolved around exposing hypocrisy in courts, rebuking unjust magistrates, defending the innocent, and restoring law to its rightful place. His teachings on justice, fairness, truth, and courage are woven into our legal DNA.

This is why every chapter begins and ends with Scripture: to remind you—and the courts—that law has a source, justice has a standard, and the fight you are entering is older than any courtroom you will ever face.

A Pro Se litigant without a compass is easily lost.
A Pro Se litigant rooted in first principles—whether moral, spiritual, or philosophical—becomes unstoppable.

That is the purpose of these verses.
Not evangelism.
Not affectation.
Orientation.

A compass at the beginning.
A reminder at the end.
A map between the two.

And a path, always, toward justice.

Foreword

A Word of Warning

This book is not for everyone.

If you are timid, thin–skinned, or afraid of losing, close these pages now. Litigation is war. The court system is not a temple of justice; it is a battlefield of procedure, prejudice, and power. If you enter that battlefield unprepared, you will be crushed.

The statistics are brutal: in federal district courts, self-represented plaintiffs win final judgment in only about **3–4 percent** of cases,[1] while self-represented defendants lose roughly **86 percent** of the time.[2]

The system is not a neutral referee. Judges may not openly resent you, but empirical research shows that the very label *"pro se"* triggers negative bias among judges, clerks, and opposing counsel.[3]

---

[1] Aaron Littman, *Empirical Patterns in Pro Se Litigation in Federal District Courts*, 98 U. Chi. L. Rev. 1707, 1707–10 (2021) (empirical study of more than 2 million federal cases; finding pro se plaintiffs prevailed in only 3–4 % of matters).
[2] Id. at pp. 1711–1713 (same dataset; noting that represented plaintiffs prevailed against pro se defendants in approximately 86 % of cases).
[3] Victor D. Quintanilla & Cheryl R. Steele, *The Signaling Effect of Pro Se Status*, 94 Ind. L.J. 1275, 1275–80 (2020) (experimental and field data showing that "pro se"

If you are reading this book looking for comfort, you will not find it here.

What you will find is doctrine. Doctrine forged in fire—tested in courtrooms where judges rig hearings and sanitize transcripts, lawyers lie without shame, and clerks can tamper with dockets and issue orders without authority. Doctrine that does not rely on reforms, kindness, or miracles. Doctrine that treats every irregularity as ammunition, every delay as confession, every insult as evidence.

But doctrine is useless without courage.

You must be willing to file when they threaten you with sanctions. You must be willing to preserve the record when they ridicule you. You must be willing to appeal, and appeal again, and never quit. You must be ready to exhaust the trial court, the appellate court, and the supreme court if necessary.

This book is written for the fearless. For those who would rather lose everything fighting on principle than compromise with corruption. For those who understand that sometimes the war is not won for yourself, but for your children—so they will not have to fight it.

If that is not you, stop now. If it is—welcome.

---

status signals incompetence and lowers perceived credibility and settlement prospects).

Why I Wrote This Book

"When you find yourself in a fair fight, your tactics are wrong."

If you are reading this, you probably already suspect that the courts are not the level playing fields they were supposed to be. You may have already seen it—maybe you lived it—the rigged rules, the unseen hands, the smirking certainty of those who believe the system belongs to them.

This book is for you.

I did not set out to become a Pro Se litigant. It never occurred to me to step into a courtroom without lawyers at my side. Like most Americans, I believed that truth mattered. That if the facts and the law were on your side, the system would work.

Then I saw the machine up close.
I saw how it chewed up ordinary people—how it *rewarded* the powerful for weaponizing the law against the very citizens it was meant to protect. I learned that survival in court is not just about being right. It is about being prepared for war.

Not a war of violence—but a war of **strategy**, **resilience**, and **truth**, fought inside a system designed to exhaust you, humiliate you, and make you quit.

This book is a guide to winning that war.

It is written from the trenches—not from a tenured professor's chair, or a glossy law office far removed from the fight. These pages are carved from real battles, real courts, real victories and defeats.
It is not just about procedures or statutes—though you will learn plenty of those.
It's about how to **think**, **fight**, and **endure** like a warrior in a world where the rules were never meant to protect you.

Most important:
I wrote this book because I believe you are **stronger than you know**.
Because you deserve to stand in the arena fully armed—with your mind sharp, your spirit unbreakable, and your cause just.

When you finish reading—and, I hope, re-reading—these pages, I want you to feel something the system fears:
Confidence.
Clarity.
Courage.

Because once you learn how the fight is really fought—you will never be helpless again.

Why You Must Prepare for War, Not Just Battle

You might imagine a single day in court—a clear winner, a just verdict, a problem solved.

But the courtroom is not a battlefield. It is a war zone.
And wars are not won in a single clash. They are won by those who are prepared to fight—and keep fighting—across many fronts, over months and years if necessary.

The enemy you are facing—whether it is a corporation, a corrupt official, or even a rogue judge—has resources. They have allies. They know how to grind you down with endless motions, obscure procedural traps, and delays designed to drain your willpower.

If you are preparing for a quick victory, you are preparing to lose.

You must prepare for **war**—not just a single **battle**.

This means building endurance into your strategy from the very beginning.
It means understanding that your first filing, your first argument, your first hearing—they are not the end. They are just the opening moves in a long campaign.

It means conserving your emotional energy, choosing your battles wisely, and seeing the bigger picture even when it feels like you are under siege.

It also means learning to take hits without breaking—because you will take hits.

But here is the truth they do not want you to know:
If you are prepared for war, you are almost impossible to defeat.

Because the system is built to break quitters, not fighters.
It expects you to give up. It depends on it.

When you refuse—when you stay calm, stay sharp, and keep coming—you change the entire dynamic. You force them to show their hand. You strip away the masks. You expose their weaknesses. And eventually, you win not just victories for yourself, but for everyone who will follow the path you helped blaze.

This is not easy work. It is not for the faint of heart.

But it is deeply worthy work.
And it is necessary.

If you are willing to prepare for war—not just battle—you will become something they cannot defeat.

You will become **unstoppable**.

How to Use This Book

(Operational Guidance for Readers and Pro Se Litigants)

This is a **field manual**, not a textbook.
Use it the way a pilot uses a checklist or a Marine uses an operations card: quickly, deliberately, and with purpose.

1. Start With the BLUF

Every chapter begins with a **Bottom Line Up Front**.
Read that first.
If the BLUF fits your situation, continue. If not, skip ahead.
This book is designed for **targeted use**, not linear study.

2. Use the Triads as Your Compass

Pro Se Legal Warfare (PSLW) doctrines operate in three modes:

- **Triad I:** Velocity · Attrition · Minimalism
- **Triad II:** Human Creativity · Cognitive Alliance · Strategic Imagination
- **Triad III:** Footnotes · Visual Law · Exhibits

Most problems are solved by applying the correct triad at the correct time.

Use this book tactically: preserve the record, control the tempo, and build every filing for the appellate court.

3. Visual Law Wins Hearings

Judges skim. Clerks skim. Lawyers bluster.
Apply the Doctrines herein to tables, timelines, and binary matrices to force the court to *see* the truth.
If your argument cannot be understood in five seconds, it may not be understood at all.

4. Stand on Your Briefs

Courtroom speech vanishes.
Verified filings survive.
Write every filing as if an appellate clerk will read it months from now—because they will.

5. Use AI as a Force Multiplier

Load the **entire electronic version** of this book into any capable AI system (ChatGPT, Claude, LLaMA, or local/offline tools) and instruct it to:

- apply the doctrines to your facts,
- draft Judicial Notices,
- generate Visual Law tables,
- build exhibit summaries,
- test your filings for structural weakness,
- produce sanctions motions using Chapter 25,
- or map appellate posture.

You supply intent and judgment; AI supplies coherence, structure, and scale.

Part I: Entering the Arena

Chapter 1 – Welcome to the Cage Match

Understanding the True Nature of Courtroom Combat

"The life of man upon earth is a warfare, and his days are like the days of a hireling." (Job 7:1)

BLUF (Bottom Line Up Front):

Court is not a church or temple of justice. It is a cage match. The sooner you see it that way, the sooner you stop asking for fairness and start fighting for survival.

The Doctrine of the Cage Match

You are not stepping into a civilized debate. You are stepping into a locked arena, surrounded by adversaries who are armed, trained, and desperate to see you beaten.

- **The judge is not neutral.** They are the referee who often favors one side and holds contempt for the other.
  - See *Liteky v. United States*, 510 U.S. 540, 555 (1994) (explaining that judicial bias may arise

during proceedings and that expressions of impatience, dissatisfaction, or partiality can be relevant to evaluating neutrality)

- **Opposing counsel cannot be assumed to be ethical.** They are paid mercenaries. They may lie, distort, and cheat because their license protects them.
- **The clerk is not your helper.** They are gatekeepers who decide which filings live, which are misfiled, and which vanish.

This is the cage match. Accept it, and you can fight on its terms.

Rules of the Doctrine

Rule 1: Stop Expecting Fairness.
Every punch they land is unfair. Expect it. Train for it. Document it.

Rule 2: Recognize the Weapons.
Lawyers often fight with lies. Judges fight with discretion. Clerks fight with suppression. Know the arsenal.

Rule 3: Fight With Doctrine, Not Emotion.
Anger is wasted. Precision is deadly. File, verify, and preserve. That is your strike.

Rule 4: Remember the Audience.
The trial judge is not your audience. The appellate record is. Build it from your first filing.

Rule 5: Accept the Blood Price.
As a Pro Se litigant you will be mocked, sanctioned, or ignored. That is the cost of entering the cage. Pay it. Keep fighting.

Tactical Applications

- When the judge smirks at you, do not argue—**note it for appeal.**
- When opposing counsel lies, do not rage—**file Judicial Notice of Misrepresentation.**
- When the clerk suppresses your motion, do not beg—**re–file with timestamp proof.**

Every dirty trick your adversary might play becomes your evidence. Every slight becomes your weapon.

Rule of War:

Court is not a temple. It is a cage. If you expect fairness, you are prey. If you accept the fight, you become a warrior.

"Fight the good fight of faith: lay hold on eternal life." (1 Tim. 6:12)

Chapter 2 – The Playing Field Is Tilted

The Reality of Judicial and Institutional Bias

"Woe to them that make wicked laws: and when they write, write injustice." (Isaiah 10:1)

BLUF (Bottom Line Up Front):

The courtroom is not level ground. The system is built to protect licensed lawyers and judges, not you.[4] If you walk in expecting equality, you have already lost.

The Doctrine of the Tilted Field

- The rules are written by lawyers, for lawyers.[5]
- Judges bend those rules to protect lawyers, not you.
- Clerks enforce rules against you, but ignore them for attorneys.

---

[4] *Turner v. Rogers*, 564 U.S. 431, 444–45 (2011) (acknowledging structural disadvantages faced by unrepresented litigants in adversarial proceedings and the risk of erroneous deprivation without adequate procedural safeguards)

[5] *Haines v. Kerner*, 404 U.S. 519, 520–21 (1972) (holding that pro se pleadings are to be construed liberally, reflecting recognition of structural imbalance between represented and unrepresented litigants)

The field is tilted. Every step uphill is harder for Pro Se. That is not paranoia—it is design.

Rules of the Doctrine

Rule 1: Assume Bias.
Judges give lawyers slack. They will give you sanctions. Accept that truth.

Rule 2: Expect Suppression.
Your filings may vanish. Their filings will be stamped instantly. Plan for obstruction.

Rule 3: Know the Double Standard.
When lawyers break rules, judges call it "discretion." When you follow rules perfectly, they will still call you "frivolous."

Rule 4: Stop Seeking Equality.
You are not on equal footing. Your strength comes from doctrine, not from the illusion of fairness.

Rule 5: Turn Tilt Into Leverage.
Every bias, delay, and double standard becomes your appellate weapon.

Tactical Applications

- **When the judge excuses lawyer misconduct:** File Judicial Notice of Double Standard. Preserve it for appeal.
- **When your filing is suppressed:** Refile with timestamp, then file Judicial Notice of Suppression.

- **When accused of frivolousness:** Attach verification and citations to statute. Make them choke on the record.
- **When denied equal treatment:** Do not argue. Document. Every denial is an exhibit for the higher court.

Rule of War:

The field is tilted. Stop whining about it. Accept it. Use it. Every step uphill is proof of your endurance and their corruption.

"God is no respecter of persons." (Acts 10:34)

Chapter 3 – The Pro Se Advantage

What You Can Do That Licensed Attorneys Cannot

"With Him is wisdom and strength: He hath counsel and understanding." (Job 12:13)

BLUF (Bottom Line Up Front):

Lawyers are chained. You are not. They fear sanctions, discipline, and reputational loss. You fight with freedom, speed, and truth. That is your advantage.

The Doctrine of the Pro Se Advantage

- Lawyers must protect their licenses. You do not have one to lose.
- Lawyers must bill hours. You can move in minutes.
- Lawyers must obey and defer to judges. You can expose judges.

- Lawyers serve clients. You serve only truth and your survival. You control your case directly, without intermediary or permission.[6]

These are not weaknesses. They are your edge.

Rules of the Doctrine

Rule 1: Freedom Is a Weapon.

You do not fear disbarment. You do not need permission. You file what must be filed.[7]

Rule 2: Speed Kills.

Lawyers drag cases for years. You can answer in hours. Velocity overwhelms them.

Rule 3: Truth Protects.

You verify every filing under penalty of perjury. Lawyers rarely do. Verification makes your word heavier than theirs.[8]

Rule 4: Precision Over Volume.

Lawyers bluff with page counts. You strike with doctrine—short, verified, undeniable.

---

[6] *Faretta v. California*, 422 U.S. 806, 834–36 (1975) (recognizing a constitutional right of self-representation grounded in personal autonomy and control over one's case)

[7] *Bounds v. Smith*, 430 U.S. 817, 821 (1977) (affirming the fundamental constitutional right of access to the courts)

[8] *Fed. R. Civ. P. 56(e)* (failure to properly address factual assertions permits the court to treat them as undisputed); See also *Celotex Corp. v. Catrett*, 477 U.S. 317, 322–23 (1986) (recognizing that failure to rebut properly supported factual assertions can justify judgment as a matter of law)

Rule 5: Pain Is Your Proof.
Sanctions do not scare you. Mockery does not stop you. Endurance is your advantage.

Tactical Applications

- **When lawyers pad filings with 50 pages:** File one 5–page verified motion with citations. Judges may sneer, but the record favors you.
- **When lawyers stall for weeks:** File your response in hours. Take control of the tempo.
- **When threatened with sanctions:** Accept them, then file Judicial Notice of Retaliation. Turn their weapon into evidence.
- **When accused of being untrained:** Say it openly—"I am not a lawyer. I am a litigant. I am sworn to truth. That is my authority."

Rule of War:

Lawyers fight with chains. You fight unchained. That is your advantage. Use it without fear.

"For the word of God is living and effectual, and more piercing than any two edged sword." (Heb. 4:12)

Part II: The Rules of Engagement

Chapter 4 – Doctrine of Command, Not Prayer

"The Lord shall fight for you, and you shall hold your peace." (Exod. 14:14)

BLUF (Bottom Line Up Front):

You do not ask biased or dishonest judges for justice. You command compliance with the law.

Why This Doctrine Matters

- Lawyers end filings with: *"Wherefore, Plaintiff prays for relief."* That phrasing is ritual—a holdover from centuries when courts mimicked churches and judges acted like priests.

- But judges are not gods. They are adjudicators—public employees bound by rules, statutes, and constitutions.[9]
- Pro Se litigants fall into a trap if they mimic lawyers and use lawyer–ritual language. It makes you look like a bad imitation of the bar, and worse, it signals **submission** to judicial whim instead of **command of law.**

Rules of the Doctrine

Rule 1: Never "pray" to a judge.
Prayer belongs to God, not to courts.

Rule 2: Use "respectfully requests" or "moves this Court to comply."
Be firm, be lawful, be clinical.

Rule 3: Always verify.
Sworn verifications carry more weight than "prayers" or conclusions.

Rule 4: Anchor in rule and statute.
Your requests should be framed as: *"Pursuant to Pa.R.C.P. 1037(b)(1), Defendant respectfully requests that the adjudicator strike the void judgment."*

Rule 5: Preserve your posture.

---

[9] *Marbury v. Madison*, 5 U.S. (1 Cranch) 137, 177 (1803) (establishing that courts are bound to apply law as written and that it is the duty of the judiciary to say what the law is)

Every filing should remind the judge: they are an adjudicator of law, not a sovereign dispensing favors.

Tactical Applications

- **Instead of:** *"Wherefore, Defendant prays this Court grant..."*
- **Write:** *"Defendant respectfully requests compliance with Rule ___ requiring ___."*
- **Instead of:** *"Comes now the Plaintiff..."*
- **Write:** *"Defendant, appearing Pro Se, files this Verified Motion pursuant to ___."*
- **Instead of:** formulaic lawyer ritual, you use **plain procedural authority**.

Why This Works

- It shocks the system: judges and clerks expect Pro Se to copy bad lawyer forms. You stand out as disciplined and different.
- It reclaims dignity: you do not act as if the judge is a priest granting blessings; you treat them as adjudicators bound by law.
- It preserves appeal: when the record shows you cited law and verified your filings, it is harder for appellate judges to dismiss you as "frivolous."

Rule of War:

Prayer belongs to God. Compliance belongs to judges. Confuse the two and you have already lost.

"Being confident of this very thing; that he, who hath begun a good work in you, will perfect it unto the day of Christ Jesus." (Phil. 1:6)

Chapter 5 – Doctrine of the Adjudicator, Not the Court

"Judge justly between the man and his brother, and the stranger that is with him." (Deut. 1:16)

BLUF (Bottom Line Up Front):

Judges are not "the Court." They are adjudicators. The Court is the record. When judges step outside statute and rule, thcy lose jurisdiction and discretion.

Why This Doctrine Matters

- Lawyers talk as though the judge *is* the Court. That myth inflates judicial power.
- The truth: **the Court is the record**—your filings, exhibits, verified notices, and transcripts.

- Judges are *temporary presiders*, nothing more. Their only lawful function is to apply statute and rule to the record.[10]

Rules of the Doctrine

Rule 1: Never equate judge with Court.
Write: "This Court" only when referring to the record, not the person. Refer to the judge as "the adjudicator."

Rule 2: Law binds, not discretion.
A judge who disregards governing statute or rule acts outside lawful authority; whether that defect is jurisdictional or reversible depends on the nature of the violation.

Jurisdictional defects render acts void, while errors within jurisdiction remain subject to appeal.

Rule 3: Ultra Vires Acts Are Null.
Orders issued in clear absence of jurisdiction or statutory authority are void ab initio; errors within jurisdiction remain subject to appellate correction.[11]

Rule 4: Your filings are the Court.
Verified motions and notices preserve the real Court, whether or not the judge obeys.

---

[10] *Ex parte Virginia*, 100 U.S. 339, 347 (1880) (holding that judicial officers are state actors bound by law and subject to constitutional limitations)
[11] *Norton v. Shelby County*, 118 U.S. 425, 442 (1886) (holding that acts performed without lawful authority are void and confer no rights)

Rule 5: Record over ritual.
Do not bow to robes. Bind them with rules.

Tactical Applications

- When a judge says "the Court has discretion," respond: "Respectfully, the Court is the record; Your Honor is the adjudicator. Statute X and Rule Y remove discretion."
- When a judge issues an order outside statute, file: *"Judicial Notice of Ultra Vires Order—void for lack of jurisdiction."*
- When opposing counsel appeals to judge's "inherent power," counter with: "Adjudicators have only what statute grants; inherent power ends at the record."

Why This Works

- **It reclaims authority.** You place "the Court" where it belongs: the record.
- **It strips myth.** Judges lose their mystical aura and stand exposed as public employees bound by rule.
- **It preserves appeal.** Every time you document ultra vires acts, you strengthen your case above.

Rule of War:

Do not mistake the adjudicator for the Court. The Court is the record. Judges who defy statute leave the Court and lose jurisdiction.

"Judge not according to the appearance, but judge just judgment." (John 7:24)

Chapter 6 – Doctrine of Jurisdictional Limits

"Thou shalt not wrest judgment: thou shalt not respect persons, nor take gifts." (Deut. 16:19)

BLUF (Bottom Line Up Front):

Jurisdiction is never waived. Orders made without jurisdiction are void ab initio—as if they never existed. Judges are adjudicators, not sovereigns. When they act in clear absencc of jurisdiction or outside statutory authority, their acts are void ab initio; ordinary legal errors within jurisdiction remain subject to appeal.

The Doctrine of Jurisdiction

- Lawyers and judges regularly misuse the word "jurisdiction."
- They talk as though a "court" is a building or a type of case, instead of what it truly is: **the lawful authority to act under statute and precedent.**
- Judges often conflate jurisdiction with **unlimited discretion** or **immunity**—pretending they can rule

however they want and hide behind the robe. That is false.

- The truth: **jurisdiction is bounded by law.**
    - If a judge acts in clear absence of jurisdiction or outside statutory authority, the act is void ab initio; errors within jurisdiction remain subject to appellate correction.
    - When jurisdiction is lacking, any purported order is void ab initio; however, prudent practice may still include appeal or collateral challenge to preserve and enforce that defect.

Rules of the Doctrine

Rule 1: Jurisdiction Is Never Waived.

- ***Steel Co. v. Citizens for a Better Environment***, 523 U.S. 83, 94–95 (1998) (holding that jurisdiction is a threshold requirement that must be established before a court may proceed to the merits).
- ***Ex parte McCardle***, 74 U.S. (7 Wall.) 506, 514 (1869) (recognizing that without jurisdiction, a court's only function is to announce the fact and dismiss the cause).

Rule 2: Ultra Vires Acts Are Void Ab Initio.

- ***Kalb v. Feuerstein***, 308 U.S. 433, 438–40 (1940) (holding that state court proceedings conducted in violation of federal statutory limits are void for lack of jurisdiction).

- A void order is not "voidable"—it is nothing. It cannot be enforced.

Rule 3: Final Orders Require Jurisdiction.

- Strict deadlines for appeal (*doctrine of laches*) apply only to final orders made with jurisdiction.
- If jurisdiction was lacking, there is no lawful final order. A void order does not become valid through time; however, prudent practice preserves the defect through appeal or collateral challenge.

Rule 4: Immunity Ends Where Jurisdiction Ends.

- Judicial immunity shields lawful rulings made within jurisdiction.
- It does not protect judges who act outside statute or in defiance of controlling law.
- ***Stump v. Sparkman***, 435 U.S. 349, 356–57 (1978) (holding that judicial immunity applies only to judicial acts within jurisdiction and does not extend to actions taken in the clear absence of all jurisdiction).

Rule 5: The Court Is Jurisdiction, Not the Judge.

- A "Court" is lawful jurisdiction embodied in the record.
- A judge is only an adjudicator. When they act in clear absence of jurisdiction, they cease to act as the Court for that specific act.

Clarification—Jurisdiction vs Error:

- Not every incorrect ruling is jurisdictional.
    - Lack of subject-matter jurisdiction → void ab initio.
    - Actions taken in clear absence of jurisdiction → void.
    - Errors within jurisdiction → reversible on appeal, not void.

The disciplined litigant distinguishes between these categories and argues them precisely.

Tactical Applications

- **When a judge rules against statute:** Immediately file *Judicial Notice of Ultra Vires Order—Void for Lack of Jurisdiction*. Preserve the defect.
- **When opposing counsel argues laches:** Respond that laches cannot bar jurisdictional challenges. Jurisdiction is never waived.
- **When the clerk enforces an ultra vires order:** File Judicial Notice of Void Order; demand compliance with higher law.
- **On appeal:** Argue jurisdiction first. If jurisdiction was lacking, higher courts cannot avoid reversal.

Why This Works

- **It reclaims the battlefield.** Judges hide behind "discretion" and "immunity." This doctrine strips both away.
- **It reframes the fight.** You are not appealing "errors." You are challenging void acts outside jurisdiction.
- **It removes laches.** Deadlines to appeal apply only to lawful final orders. Void orders never become final.
- **It exposes corruption.** Every ultra vires ruling becomes evidence that the judge was not acting as the Court.

Rule of War:

Jurisdiction is not just assumed by locale. It is proven. Judges who defy statute or precedent leave the Court. They act without jurisdiction, without power, and without law.

"There is no power but from God: and those that are, are ordained of God." (Rom. 13:1)

Chapter 7 – Doctrine of Love for the Law

"Better is a little with justice, than great revenues with iniquity." (Prov. 16:8)

BLUF (Bottom Line Up Front):

If you do not love the law, you will quit when it turns against you. If you love it, you will endure, even when every judge, lawyer, and clerk betrays it.

The Doctrine of Loving the Law

- The law is not the judge. The law is not the lawyer. The law is not the clerk.
- The law is the statutes, the rules, and the Constitution.[12]
- The system twists it. The adjudicators ignore it. But the law remains.

---

[12] *Marbury v. Madison*, 5 U.S. (1 Cranch) 137, 177 (1803) (law governs the exercise of judicial power)

- If you hate the law because they pervert it, you will burn out. If you love it, you will fight longer than they can imagine.

Rules of the Doctrine

Rule 1: Separate the Law from the System.
The law is pure. The system is corrupt. Never confuse the two.

Rule 2: Anchor Yourself in Statute.
When everything feels rigged, hold to the written word. It cannot be erased.

Rule 3: Love the Weapon, Not the Wielder.
Judges misuse the law like a club. Lawyers twist it into lies. You wield it cleanly.

Rule 4: Let Love Replace Fear.
If you love the law, you no longer fear judges or sanctions. You fear only betraying the law itself.

Rule 5: Carry It into Battle.
The law will not protect you in every fight. But your love for it will sustain you when the system throws you to the ground.

Tactical Applications

- **When a judge sneers at your citations:** Remember—the law is not him. File Judicial Notice and preserve the rule anyway.

- **When lawyers mock your use of statutes:** Remember—the law is not them. Verification will outlast their words.
- **When clerks suppress your filings:** Remember—the law is not the docket. Refile and document. The record will live beyond them.
- **When you are exhausted:** Read the Constitution, the rules, the statutes. Love them. They are your only honest ally.

Rule of War:

If you love the law, you cannot be broken. If you have contempt for it, you will be lost.

"All things that are reproved, are made manifest by the light." (Eph. 5:13)

Chapter 8 – Doctrine of Mission Clarity

"O how have I loved thy law, O Lord! it is my meditation all the day." (Ps. 118:97)

BLUF (Bottom Line Up Front):

If you do not know why you are in court, you will be pushed, mocked, and broken. Judges and lawyers thrive on confusion. Mission clarity keeps you steady when everything else is chaos.

The Doctrine of Mission Clarity

- Court is distraction by design. Lawyers bury you in paper. Judges may bait you with condescension and insults. Clerks frustrate you with suppression.
- If you do not have a clear mission, you will start chasing rabbits and forget why you came.
- Your mission is simple: **preserve the record, enforce the law, survive to appeal.** Everything else is noise.

Rules of the Doctrine

Rule 1: Define Your Mission Before You File.
Write it down: *What is the relief I seek? What statute or rule compels it?*

Rule 2: Filter Every Move Through the Mission.
If a filing or argument does not serve the mission, it is dead weight.

Rule 3: Expect Diversion.
Judges may and will insult you. Lawyers will provoke you. Clerks will delay you. Recognize distraction for what it is: off–mission interference.

Rule 4: Anchor in Law, Not Emotion.
Your mission is to enforce statute and precedent, not to vent. Emotion is fuel, not evidence.

Rule 5: Mission Ends in the Record.
If it is not in the record, it did not happen.[13] Your mission is to build a record that wins later, not applause that fades now.

Tactical Applications

- **When the judge calls you "frivolous":** Do not argue. Restate your mission: *"This motion cites Rule ___. The record will reflect compliance."*

---

[13] *United States v. Wade*, 388 U.S. 218, 224–25 (1967) (emphasizing the importance of preserving events in the record for appellate review)

- **When opposing counsel piles on insults:** Ignore the noise. File, verify, and preserve. Your mission is not to fight them—it is to lock the record.
- **When clerks stall your filings:** Do not rage. Document and refile. The mission is preservation, not popularity.
- **When you are tempted to chase every injustice:** Ask: *Does this serve my mission? Or is it a trap?*

Why This Works

- Lawyers want you confused. Judges want you reactive. Clerks want you exhausted.
- Mission clarity makes you unshakable. You always know why you are there, and they cannot move you off it.
- On appeal, the mission speaks for you. A clean, focused record stands taller than any courtroom insult.

Rule of War:

If you do not know your mission, they will write it for you. Know it, live it, and never move off it.

"Think not that I am come to destroy the law, or the prophets: I am not come to destroy, but to fulfill." (Matt. 5:17)

Chapter 9 – Doctrine of the Written Record

"Write the vision, and make it plain upon tables: that he that readeth it may run." (Hab. 2:2)

BLUF (Bottom Line Up Front):

Your filings are your voice. Judges will interrupt you. Lawyers will talk over you. Clerks will muffle you. But the written record cannot be shouted down. It is your only weapon that survives.

The Doctrine of the Written Record

- Courtroom words vanish. Written words remain.[14]
- Judges know this, which is why they try to corner you in live hearings.
- Lawyers know this, which is why they bait you into arguing instead of filing.

[14] *Anderson v. City of Bessemer City*, 470 U.S. 564, 573–74 (1985) (appellate review is confined to the record developed below)

- The truth is simple: **a short, verified brief is stronger than an hour of argument.**[15]

Rules of the Doctrine

Rule 1: Say Less, Write More.
Never waste breath when a filing will do.

Rule 2: Verification Is Power.
Attach your oath. Lawyers almost never do. That makes your brief heavier than theirs.

Rule 3: Brevity Wins.
Ten tight pages beat fifty bloated ones. Judges read what they cannot avoid—short filings.

Rule 4: Always Stand on the Record.
In hearings, say: *"I stand on my briefs."* This locks the judge into the filing.

Rule 5: Build for Appeal.
Remember: the appellate court reads the record. They do not hear the shouting. They see the brief.

Tactical Applications

- **When a judge demands oral argument:** Keep it short. Repeat: *"The filing speaks for itself."* Force the record to stand.

---

[15] *Fed. R. Civ. P. 56(e)* (failure to properly address factual assertions permits the court to treat them as undisputed)

- **When lawyers flood with 50–page motions:** File 5 pages, verified, with citations. Let them drown in their own volume.
- **When insulted in open court:** Do not spar. Preserve. File a Judicial Notice after. The brief lives, the insult dies.
- **When unsure what to say:** Say nothing. Say: *"The record reflects my position."* That phrase ends traps.
    - Example: During a sanctions threat, saying nothing until the judge demanded a reply forced the court to confront its own overreach on the transcript.

Why This Works

- Oral argument is theater. Written briefs are ammunition.
- Judges can ignore your words in the moment, but they cannot erase a verified filing.
- Appeals live on the record. If you master the written record, you control the fight above.

Rule of War:

The tongue is wind. The record is iron. Stand on your briefs and let the record fight for you.

"Let your speech be: yea, yea: no, no: and that which is over and above these, is of evil." (Matt. 5:37)

Chapter 10 – Doctrine of Appellate Vision

"Thus saith the Lord, the God of Israel: Write all the words that I have spoken to thee in a book." (Jer. 30:2)

BLUF (Bottom Line Up Front):

You are not fighting for the trial judge.[16] You are fighting for the appellate record. Every filing, every objection, every notice is aimed at the higher court, not the hostile adjudicator in front of you.

The Doctrine of Appellate Vision

- Trial court is a battlefield of noise. Appeals are decided on paper.
- Judges may mock you, lawyers may provoke you, clerks may bury you—but appellate panels will never see that theater.
- They will see only what is in the record: the motions, the notices, the verifications, the transcript.

---

[16] *Cardinale v. Louisiana*, 394 U.S. 437, 438 (1969) (issues not raised below are not preserved for appellate review)

- Your vision must be fixed upward from the start.

Rules of the Doctrine

Rule 1: Build the Record from Day One.
Assume every filing will be read by an appellate clerk months later. Write for them, not the trial judge.

Rule 2: Preserve Every Error.
Object, file, and notice. If you do not preserve it below, you lose it above.[17]

Rule 3: Precision Over Passion.
Appellate panels do not care how angry you were. They care if statute and precedent were preserved.

Rule 4: Documentation Is Appeal.
No transcript, no appeal. No notice, no appeal. No verified record, no appeal.

Rule 5: Appeal Is the True Audience.
The trial judge is a gatekeeper. The appellate panel is the real jury.

Tactical Applications

- **When insulted by a judge:** Do not argue. File Judicial Notice of Judicial Conduct. Appellate courts will see the filing, not the insult.

---

[17] *Hormel v. Helvering*, 312 U.S. 552, 556 (1941) (appellate courts generally do not consider issues not raised in the trial court)

- **When lawyers lie in hearing:** Do not spar. Preserve with transcript request and Judicial Notice of Misrepresentation.
- **When rulings ignore statute:** File Motion to Strike or Vacate, even if denied. Denial preserves the issue.
- **When exhausted:** Remember the mission. The appellate court is blind to emotion. It sees only the record.

Why This Works

- Trial courts run on theater. Appeals run on evidence.
- When you fight for the appellate record, you strip power from the trial judge and hand it to the higher court.
- Lawyers stumble here. They argue to trial judges for approval. You fight for appeal. That difference is decisive.

Rule of War:

The trial judge is noise. The appellate record is signal. Fix your vision upward, and let the record speak for you.

"Pilate answered: What I have written, I have written." (John 19:22)

Chapter 11 – Doctrine of the Warrior's Posture

"Call upon me, and I will answer thee: and will shew thee great and mighty things, which thou knowest not." (Jer. 33:3)

BLUF (Bottom Line Up Front):

You must fight with the spirit of a warrior but the discipline of a litigator. Rage will burn you out. Fear will paralyze you. Balance is survival, because only disciplined conduct preserves the record that appellate courts review.

The Doctrine of the Warrior's Posture

- Court is combat. You cannot enter timidly. You must be willing to take blows and keep standing.
- But court is also record–building. You cannot swing wildly. Every move must be precise.
- The balance is posture: warrior in spirit, litigator in execution.

Rules of the Doctrine

Rule 1: Do Not Hate.
Hatred clouds vision. Your fight is with corruption, not with yourself.

Rule 2: Do Not Fear.
Fear is what judges and lawyers feed on. They cannot touch you if you stay anchored in law.

Rule 3: Fight With Discipline.
Every filing, every objection, every notice must be tactical. No wasted motion.

Rule 4: Endure the Pain.
Sanctions, insults, and delays will come. Endurance is proof of your strength.

Rule 5: Balance Spirit and Strategy.
Let the warrior drive you forward, but let the litigator aim your strikes.

Tactical Applications

- **When insulted in open court:** Do not lash out. Stay calm. File Judicial Notice later. The warrior absorbs the blow; the litigator records it.
- **When sanctioned:** Do not panic. Accept it. File Motion for Reconsideration or Judicial Notice of Retaliation. Pain is fuel.

- **When exhausted:** Re–read your mission statement. The warrior remembers why he fights; the litigator knows how.
- **When tempted to hate:** Redirect it. Focus on rules, statutes, and precision filings. Hatred wastes energy.

Why This Works

- Judges expect fear. Lawyers expect rage. When you show neither, they lose control.
- Balanced posture makes you unpredictable. You cannot be baited, and you cannot be broken.
- Appeals are won by records, not emotions. But only warriors endure long enough to build those records.

Rule of War:

Be a warrior in spirit, a litigator in execution. Courage fuels you. Discipline saves you.

"For we walk by faith, and not by sight." (2 Cor. 5:7)

Chapter 12 – Doctrine of First Blood

"The Lord is my light and my salvation, whom shall I fear?" (Ps. 27:1)

BLUF (Bottom Line Up Front):

Most cases are won or lost in the first 90 days. Early moves decide momentum, credibility, and whether you are seen as prey or as a threat.

The Doctrine of First Blood

- Litigation is not won at trial. It is won in the first filings, the first motions, the first signals you send.
- The system is always watching: How do you write? How do you file? Do you meet deadlines? Do you look dangerous, or do you look weak?
- The first 90 days determine whether they come at you with arrogance—or with caution.

Rules of the Doctrine

Rule 1: File Clean and Deadly.
Your complaint or petition must be precise, professional, and built against dismissal.

Rule 2: Anticipate the Attack.
Early motions to dismiss are certain. Draft so that dismissal is dangerous for them.

Rule 3: Control the Frame.
Set the narrative with your first filings. Define the facts, the law, and the issues on your terms.

Rule 4: Document Everything.
From day one, build a complete record: docket copies, emails, letters, timelines. If it is not documented, it does not exist.

Rule 5: Early Wins Matter.
Even small victories—meeting deadlines flawlessly, beating back dismissal, forcing discovery—tilt the field in your favor.

Tactical Applications

- **Drafting the Complaint:**
  Use Bell Atlantic Corp. v. Twombly and Ashcroft v. Iqbal standards: plead plausible, non-conclusory, fact-supported claims tied to specific causes of action.[18]

---

[18] *Bell Atlantic Corp. v. Twombly*, 550 U.S. 544, 555–57 (2007) (holding that a complaint must state a claim that is plausible on its face, not merely conceivable); *Ashcroft v. Iqbal*, 556 U.S. 662, 678–79 (2009) (clarifying that conclusory allegations are not entitled to the assumption of truth and that factual content must permit a reasonable inference of liability).

- **Facing Motions to Dismiss:**
Prepare before they file. Cite controlling standards. Force the judge to violate precedent to dismiss.

- **Record–Building:**
Maintain your own docket. Save every filing, email, and communication. In *United States v. Wade*, the Supreme Court stressed the importance of the early record. Build it now.[19]

- **Early Psychological Warfare:**
Meeting every deadline, filing flawless briefs, and documenting suppression rattles opposing counsel. They probe for weakness—deny it to them.

- **Checklist for the First 90 Days:**
    - File a professional, specific, plausible complaint.
    - Anticipate motions to dismiss and draft against them.
    - Keep a complete private docket and case file.
    - Respond promptly and properly to every filing.
    - Communicate firmly, without emotion.
    - Focus on the appellate record, not just the fight in front of you.

Why This Works

[19] *United States v. Wade*, 388 U.S. 218, 224–25 (1967) (emphasizing the importance of preserving events in the record for later review and adversarial testing)

- Early credibility shifts the entire case.
- Judges and lawyers decide who you are in the opening moves—soft target or hardened fighter.
- Momentum once lost is hard to regain. Momentum gained is easy to maintain.

Rule of War:

First blood decides the battle. Strike clean in the first 90 days, and you control the war that follows.

"Put you on the full armor of God, that you may be able to stand against the deceits of the devil." (Eph. 6:11)

Part III: The Battle Plan

Chapter 13 – Doctrine of Measuring the Field

"The horse is prepared against the day of battle: but the Lord giveth safety." (Prov. 21:31)

BLUF (Bottom Line Up Front):

Before you can win, you must see. Every courtroom is a battlefield with its own terrain, culture, and players. Victory begins with measuring—the judge, the opposing counsel, the room itself, and your own footing.

The Doctrine of Measuring the Field

- Small acts in the opening moments decide the dynamics of a case.
- Judges reveal themselves in temperament and tone.
- Lawyers expose their arrogance or insecurity early.
- Courtrooms have atmospheres—disciplined or sloppy—that shape the fight.
- Your first task is not to conquer, but to measure.

- Example: In one hearing, a judge who joked about "moving things along" at the expense of procedure revealed more bias in ten seconds than in fifty pages of orders.

Rules of the Doctrine

Rule 1: Measure the Judge.
Test for temperament, bias, and respect for procedure. A judge who flinches at small rules is weak; one who enforces evenly still honors the robe.

Rule 2: Measure Opposing Counsel.
Arrogance is their tell. Sloppiness on rules, emotional outbursts, or deference to the judge's politics reveal vulnerabilities.

Rule 3: Measure the Room.
Courtrooms breathe. Loose rooms allow abuse but create appellate error; strict rooms bind you but also bind the judge.

Rule 4: Use Small Acts to Shift Dynamics.
Rise firmly, speak formally, object cleanly, accept rulings with composure. Each small act reshapes perception of you.

Rule 5: Measure, Do not Judge.
You are gathering intelligence, not drawing final conclusions. Stay fluid. Adapt as the wind shifts.

Tactical Applications

- **Measuring the Judge:**
    - Speak formally, watch eyes and tone.
    - File timely, raise clean objections. Gauge reactions.
- **Measuring Opposing Counsel:**
    - Let them talk. Watch for overconfidence or hostility.
    - Press small procedural points to see if they snap.
- **Measuring the Courtroom:**
    - Observe the clerk and reporter.
    - Note the presence of observers.
    - Read the level of discipline—loose or tight.
- **Shifting Dynamics with Small Acts:**
    - Always rise before speaking.
    - Always address "Your Honor."
    - Object briefly, then withdraw.
    - Stand on your briefs, not on improvisation.
    - Accept rulings with: *"Noted for the record, Your Honor."*

Why This Works

- Measuring reveals the hidden currents: bias, arrogance, culture.
- Small acts carry disproportionate weight. They mark you as disciplined, not desperate.
- The system watches you in these moments. When you measure well, you unsettle them without saying a word.

Rule of War:

You cannot fight the battle you wish for. You must fight the battle you are in. First see the field. Then take it.

"I have fought a good fight, I have finished my course, I have kept the faith." (2 Tim. 4:7)

Chapter 14 – Doctrine of Provocation

"A deceitful balance is an abomination before the Lord: and a just weight is his will." (Prov. 11:1)

BLUF (Bottom Line Up Front):

Judges and lawyers reveal themselves when provoked. Your goal is not to fight with emotion, but to draw misconduct into the open and preserve it on the record.[20]

The Doctrine of Provocation

- Courtroom corruption thrives in the shadows. Exposure destroys it.
- You do not provoke with insults or rage. You provoke with discipline: clean objections, procedural enforcement, and silence at key moments.
- When they snap, interrupt, or violate procedure, the record captures it. That record is your weapon.

---

[20] See Liteky v. United States, 510 U.S. 540, 555 (1994) (judicial conduct during proceedings may become part of the record relevant to bias or procedural irregularity)

- Example 1: When counsel snapped at a calm objection and blurted “we don’t need to follow that rule,” the transcript itself became the proof of misconduct.
- Example 2: When a judge cut off an objection mid–sentence, the litigant paused, noted it for the record, and later filed Judicial Notice—turning a silencing attempt into appellate ammunition.

Provocation must always remain within procedural bounds; otherwise it becomes sanctionable conduct rather than record-building.

Rules of the Doctrine

Rule 1: Provoke With Procedure.
Enforce rules strictly. Demand order of motions. Object cleanly. Watch who resists.

Rule 2: Never Provoke With Emotion.
Anger feeds them. Discipline starves them.

Rule 3: Trap Them Into Error.
Force the judge or opposing counsel to overreach. Then preserve their misstep in the record.

Rule 4: Preserve, Do not Argue.
Once misconduct shows, stop. Enter Judicial Notice later. Do not fight beyond the record.

Rule 5: Provoke for Appeal.
Your target is not the trial judge's conscience—it is the appellate panel's eyes.

Tactical Applications

- **With Judges:**
    - Raise small procedural objections early. See if they flinch or snap.
    - If they deny your right to speak as the moving party, object once, then preserve.
    - If they ignore pending motions, object briefly: *"Objection, motions remain pending and must be adjudicated first."* Then withdraw.
- **With Opposing Counsel:**
    - Let them overtalk. Let them sneer. Stay silent until they cross procedure, then object.
    - File Judicial Notice of Misconduct. Their arrogance becomes your exhibit.
- **With Courtroom Dynamics:**
    - Use silence to force them to fill the void. When they over–explain, they reveal weakness.
    - A single calm objection after a flurry of lawyer chatter is devastating.

Why This Works

- Corrupt judges and lawyers are not disciplined fighters. They rely on you to break first.
- When you stay calm and provoke through procedure, they reveal bias and misconduct for you.
- The record becomes your ally—showing who lost control and who stayed disciplined.

Rule of War:

Do not fight to vent. Fight to provoke. Draw misconduct into the light, preserve it, and let the record destroy them.

"Which of you, having a mind to build a tower, doth not first sit down and reckon the charges, that he hath wherewithal to finish it?" (Luke 14:28)

Chapter 15 – Doctrine of Precision Strikes

"There is no wisdom, there is no prudence, there is no counsel against the Lord." (Prov. 21:30)

BLUF (Bottom Line Up Front):

Your written filings are not paperwork. They are weapons. A single precise submission, verified and sharp, can cut deeper than hours of oral argument or fifty bloated pages from opposing counsel.

The Doctrine of Precision Strikes

- Judges skim, clerks file, and appellate courts read. Written words outlive the noise of hearings.
- Lawyers rely on volume. You rely on accuracy.
- Precision strikes mean short, disciplined filings that carry law, fact, and verification—nothing more, nothing less.
- Every submission should feel like a clean blow, not wasted motion.

- Example: A five–page verified motion citing one controlling statute forced a ruling that opposing counsel's forty–page brief could not prevent.

Rules of the Doctrine

Rule 1: File Short, File Sharp.
Ten clean pages beat fifty messy ones. Judges read what they cannot avoid.

Rule 2: Verification Is Ammunition.
Sworn filings weigh more than lawyer rhetoric. Verification gives your words force.

Rule 3: Anchor in Law and Fact.
Cite statute, cite precedent, state facts. Do not fill space with adjectives or emotion.

Rule 4: Control the Narrative.
Frame the issues before they do. A precise motion defines the battlefield.

Rule 5: One Strike, One Purpose.
Each filing should aim at a single objective: dismiss, compel, vacate, preserve. Do not scatter fire.

Tactical Applications

- **Complaints and Petitions:** Draft for survival. Apply *Twombly–Iqbal* pleading standards: plausible, non-conclusory, fact-supported claims tied to specific causes of action.
- **Motions:** Keep to the core relief. Do not argue ten points. Strike on the strongest law.
- **Judicial Notices:** Use sparingly, but precisely. Each should preserve a single, undeniable defect.
- **Objections:** File cleanly, even if overruled. Each objection lays another stone in the appellate road.
- **Appeals:** Build from day one with precise filings. The appellate court will see your discipline.

Why This Works

- Judges have little patience. They respect brevity, not rambling.
- Lawyers bluff with volume. You win with precision.
- Appellate courts live on the record. Precision filings survive; courtroom chatter does not.
- Precision marks you as dangerous. It tells the system: you are not flailing—you are striking.

Rule of War:

One precise strike is deadlier than a hundred wasted motions. File sharp. File clean. File to kill.

"For the weapons of our warfare are not carnal, but mighty to God unto the pulling down of fortifications." (2 Cor. 10:4)

Part IV: Weapons of War (Core Doctrines)

Chapter 16 – Doctrine of Litigation As Signal Recovery

"For God is judge: one he putteth down, and another he lifteth up." (Ps. 75:7)

BLUF (Bottom Line Up Front):

Litigation is not warfare itself. It is a structured, rule–bound, input–output system and a battlefield.

Litigation operates on two planes at once:

Structurally, it is a rule-bound system—predictable, codified, and governed by procedure.

Operationally, it is conducted by human actors who behave as combatants—biased, strategic, and often adversarial.

The disciplined litigant understands both:

- you engage the system as an engineer, and the actors as adversaries.
- Confusing the two leads to defeat; mastering both creates control.

The best litigation (battlefield) strategies do not mimic combat—they mimic systems engineering.

The Pro Se litigant who understands litigation as signal processing, not adversarial combat, holds the decisive advantage.

Key Takeaways

- Litigation is **rules–based**, not chaos–driven. It behaves more like a legal machine than a battlefield.
- Most losses occur because litigants treat the courtroom like a fight, not a formal process.
- Winning is less about emotion or identity, and more about **procedural coherence and legal syntax.**
- Pro Se litigants can dominate institutional actors by treating filings like **commands**, not like persuasive essays.
- Legal distortion (e.g., docket flooding, lawfare) is best countered with **signal recovery**—precision filings that simplify, clarify, and trap.
- Courts cannot easily rule against **clean, unrebutted, fact–anchored procedural frameworks.**

Core Doctrine

Litigation is not an act of warfare.
It is an act of structured assertion inside a **governed operating system.**

Warfare begins with chaos. Litigation begins with form.

War is unpredictability at scale.
Litigation is **predictability disrupted by people**.

Most litigation is lost not because the rules failed, but because they were never properly invoked.

The System as a Codebase

Litigation is a coded system. Its rules behave like executable commands.

- **Pa.R.C.P. 1035.3(d)**: Failure to rebut material facts = **judicial admission**
- **Pa.R.C.P. 212.1(e)**: No pretrial submissions without formal schedule = **invalid trial posture**
- **18 Pa.C.S. § 4904**: Verification clause = **statutory affidavit**
- ***Mathews v. Eldridge***, 424 U.S. 319, 334–35 (1976) (establishing procedural due process as a balancing test based on context, risk of error, and governmental interest)
- Due process = **context–dependent but testable**

These rules are not guidance. They are **syntax**. When triggered correctly, the court must respond.

Litigation as Signal Processing

The true danger to a corrupt or overwhelmed system is not defiance—it is coherence.
Lawfare is noise. Correct filings are signal.

The well–prepared litigant does not raise volume—they **reduce distortion**.

- A concise Judicial Notice is more powerful than 50 pages of accusations.
- A motion rooted in unrebutted facts cannot be dismissed without exposure.
- A strategically–timed filing can halt an opponent's narrative and collapse judicial inertia.

The courtroom does not need drama. It needs logic that cannot be ignored.

How to Think Like a Systems Operator, Not a Combatant

- Write with clean syntax, not emotional force.
- File as if your document is a switch. If it is flipped, the court must act.
- Seek no praise. Court filings are **logic bombs**, not declarations.
- Never explain. Prove.
- Never respond in full. **Respond where it hurts.**
- Do not let your opponent drag you into noise. File once, file right, file fatal.

When the System Violates Itself

Litigation is not fair. But it is still **trackable**.

When corruption occurs:

- Do not escalate emotionally.
- Force record closure.
- Highlight contradictions.
- Use **verified facts**, statutes, and judicial silence to trap.

Courts cannot refute a clean record without exposing themselves.

Rules of the Doctrine

Rule 1: The courtroom is not a chaotic battlefield.
It is a processor. Feed it clean inputs.

Rule 2: Make it easier for the court to rule for you than against you.

Rule 3: Silence is not defeat.
It is the space where unrebutted facts become law.[21]

Rule 4: Never fight noise with noise.
Cut through with signal.

---

[21] See ***Fed. R. Civ. P. 56(e)***; ***Celotex Corp. v. Catrett***, 477 U.S. 317, 322–23 (1986)

Summary

Litigation is not combat.
It is correction.

The system is imperfect, but its structure still favors those who engage with surgical precision.

The strongest filings are not emotional. They are unignorable.
They do not provoke a ruling.
They **leave the court no choice**.

Litigation is not war.
It is signal recovery.
Be the signal.

Rule of War:

File with the clarity the system cannot corrupt—
and even corruption must yield to coherence.

"He that hath ears to hear, let him hear." (Matt. 11:15)

Chapter 17 – Doctrine of the Bellwether

"A just man shall be in everlasting remembrance." (Ps. 112:6)

BLUF (Bottom Line Up Front):

The most decisive victories are often won before the judge rules and before the hearing occurs.
This is the ***Bellwether Doctrine***: establishing a record so procedurally sound, so legally coherent, and so unrebutted that the court cannot proceed against you without compromising its own legitimacy.

Key Takeaways

- **Bellwether filings shape the legal climate of the case**—they signal strength and force opposing parties and courts to act within constrained boundaries.
- You can win *before* a ruling by anchoring the record with unrebutted fact, verified filings, and precision citations.

- Judges often delay ruling because they are **assessing posture, not just arguments**—they observe who has control, not just who has merit.
- Silence by opposing counsel in response to verified notices, unrebutted affidavits, or procedural objections **functions as confession** under court rules.
- The doctrine is not about theater. It is about **preemptive legitimacy**—filing so cleanly and completely that the court must concede without conflict.

Core Doctrine

Litigation is not a battle of wits at the podium.
It is a battle of posture on the record.

The Bellwether Doctrine holds that:

"The side that frames the narrative, owns the record, and compels procedural compliance before a single ruling is issued—has already won."

This means building:

- Verified Judicial Notices with statutory authority
- Motions that cite unrebutted material fact under **Pa.R.C.P. 1035.3(d)**
- Procedural objections under **Pa.R.C.P. 1028(c)**, **212.1(e)**, or **Rule 208.3(b)**
- A written trail the court cannot ignore without risking appellate reversal

You are not asking the judge for permission to win.
You are ***building the record so well that the judge cannot ethically deny you.***

Pre–Ruling Dominance: Signs You are Executing the Doctrine

Action	Signal
Verified filing is not rebutted	Opponent has conceded fact under Rule 1035.3(d) or Rule 208.3(b)
No counter–affidavits are filed	Your version becomes the official narrative
Opponent floods docket with unnecessary trial documents	You have forced them into procedural theater
Judge stops questioning your filings and only asks about tone or format	You have won the substance
Rulings are delayed, then mimic your proposed order language	You are shaping the ruling itself

---

Law Behind the Doctrine

- **Pa.R.C.P. 1035.3(d)**: *"All material facts set forth in the motion are deemed admitted when not properly controverted by affidavit or otherwise."*

- **Pa.R.C.P. 208.3(b)**: Unopposed motions may be granted as of right.
- ***Commonwealth v. McClelland***, 233 A.3d 717, 734–35 (Pa. 2020) (courts must base decisions on competent evidence, not presumption or speculation).
- ***Mathews v. Eldridge***, 424 U.S. 319, 334–35 (1976)

These principles all favor the prepared Pro Se litigant who understands the value of ***winning the paper, not the podium.***

How to Execute the Doctrine

1. **File with Precision**
   - Every motion should cite statute or rule in the first sentence.
   - Verify all filings under **18 Pa.C.S. § 4904** to create sworn statements.
2. **Create Procedural Entrapment**
   - Demand rulings in sequence.
   - File a **Judicial Notice of Procedural Bar** if the court attempts to skip your motion.
3. **Time Your Silence**
   - After filing a dispositive motion, do not follow with more filings unless forced.
   - Let the silence amplify. Your opponent will overreach.

4. **Include Proposed Orders**
    - Give the court an easy way out: a simple, clean proposed order that reflects procedural truth.
    - Courts often adopt well–framed orders verbatim when cornered by record precision.

Rules of the Doctrine

Rule 1: Treat the Courtroom as a Processor, Not an Arena.

Litigation runs on inputs, rules, and outputs. When you feed the system clean, verified inputs, you force lawful outputs—even when humans resist them.

Rule 2: Structure Filings so the Court Can More Easily Rule for You Than Against You.

A filing built on statute, verification, and binary framing becomes the path of least resistance. Courts follow the easiest coherent option.

Rule 3: Silence Is Not Absence—It Is Conversion.

When you submit verified fact and the opponent does not rebut, silence converts your fact into judicial truth by operation of rule.

Rule 4: Never Counter Noise With Noise—Answer Distortion With Coherence.

Opponents flood the docket to create signal loss. You answer with one precise, verified filing that restores clarity and traps the contradiction.

Rule 5: File as if Each Document Is a Switch—Once Flipped, It Forces the System to Respond.

Every verified motion or notice should be structured as an executable command: if X is true and unrebutted, the only lawful outcome is Y.

Summary

The Bellwether Doctrine is not a tactic. It is a mindset.
It is the decision to shape the field so decisively that the hearing becomes irrelevant.

You win not by what you say in court.
You win by **what is already in the record** when you walk in.
You win when silence becomes your opponent's confession.
You win when the court ***cannot proceed without breaking the system it was sworn to uphold.***

Win before ruling.
Own the record.
Be the bellwether.

Rule of War:

Cut through the noise; the court always follows the clearest signal.

"By their fruits you shall know them." (Matt. 7:16)

Chapter 18 – Doctrine of the Procedural Guillotine

"The wicked shall be cut off from the earth: and the unjust shall be taken away from it." (Prov. 2:22)

BLUF (Bottom Line Up Front):

The most effective way to end a case is not by winning an argument. It is by building a record the court cannot contradict without exposing itself.

The **Procedural Guillotine** is the strategic use of unrebutted facts, verified filings, and judicial delay to **close the case logically**—before the court ever rules.

Key Takeaways

- Courts are bound by unrebutted facts under **Pa.R.C.P. 1035.3(d)** and equivalent federal and state rules.
- Silence is not just absence, it becomes procedural admission when the record is structured under governing rules to treat it that way.

- When the court delays but does not deny, time becomes a blade—sharpened by procedural weight.
- Filings that are verified, unrebutted, and entered into a dormant record eventually create **a trap the court cannot escape** without admitting bias.
- The goal is not speed. The goal is structure that will hold up *even if* the case goes sideways.

Core Doctrine

The guillotine is not a weapon. It is a frame.

Once set, it does not need to move quickly. It only needs gravity.

The **Procedural Guillotine** is the sequence of:

1. Verified factual filings,
2. Statutory or rule–anchored objections,
3. Judicial notice of silence or delay, and
4. A final motion that ***demands closure based on the court's own inaction.***

The court cannot step over the blade once it is lowered. It can only step into it.

Mechanics and Rules

1. **File Verified Motions and Facts**

- Use **18 Pa.C.S. § 4904** or equivalent verification language to elevate pleadings into sworn statements.
- Include citations to **Pa.R.C.P. 1035.3(d)** or Fed. R. Civ. P. 56(e): *"Failure to controvert = deemed admitted."*

2. **Judicial Silence**
   - After filing, wait. If no response comes within the prescribed time, file a **Judicial Notice of Silence and Unrebutted Record**.
   - This sets the trap. Courts are now forced to rule against facts they have implicitly accepted.
3. **Motion for Final Consideration**
   - Once the record is closed, file a motion styled: *"Request for Final Disposition Based on Judicial Silence and Unrebutted Material Record."*
4. **Appeal–Ready Posture**
   - If the court still ignores, file a Judicial Notice that preservation is complete and **any adverse ruling will trigger appeal or federal review.**

Rule Trigger Examples:

- **Pa.R.C.P. 1035.3(d)**: All facts deemed admitted
- **Pa.R.C.P. 208.3(b)**: Unopposed motions may be granted as of right

- ***Commonwealth v. McClelland***, 233 A.3d 717 (Pa. 2020) (courts must base decisions on competent evidence, not presumption or speculation).
- ***Mathews v. Eldridge***, 424 U.S. 319, 334–35 (1976) (procedural due process is measured by the private interest, risk of erroneous deprivation, value of additional safeguards, and governmental interest).

Execution Checklist

- Was the motion verified?
- Was the factual record unrebutted?
- Has the opposition remained silent?
- Has the court failed to rule?
- Was a Judicial Notice filed documenting all the above?

If yes to all five, the guillotine is armed.

Now, wait.
And when the court tries to rule against the structure, **the record cuts back.**

Rules of the Doctrine

Rule 1: Verified facts carry weight the court cannot ignore.

Unrebutted, they descend with the force of judgment.

Rule 2: Judicial silence is not delay.

It is acceptance of the record you built unless contradicted by rule or affidavit.

Rule 3: A procedural trap gains power from stillness, not motion.

Do not force the blade. Let gravity sharpen it.

Rule 4: Build the record so cleanly that the court cannot rule against you without exposing itself.

Structure is the weapon—not volume.

Rule 5: When the record is complete, stop filing.

The guillotine drops only when you step back and let silence do the cutting.

Summary

Litigation is not a race.
It is **a sequence of structure, silence, and procedural gravity.**

The Procedural Guillotine does not swing.
It drops—once the system steps underneath it.

Set it clean. Set it early.
Then let silence do the cutting.

Rule of War:

Give the rule, build the record, set the deadline—and then step back. When silence meets structure, the blade falls on its own.

"Every plant which my heavenly Father hath not planted, shall be rooted up." (Matt. 15:13)

Chapter 19 – Doctrine of the Sur–Reply

"Answer not a fool according to his folly, lest thou be made like him." (Prov. 26:4)

BLUF (Bottom Line Up Front):

The final word is not just a rebuttal. It is a strategic overwrite.
The **Sur–Reply Doctrine** is the controlled use of final response to reframe a dispute, neutralize the opponent's closing argument, and anchor the judge's last impression before ruling.

Key Takeaways

- A sur–reply is not a right, it is a **tactical privilege** that should only be used when an opponent introduces new arguments, misstates law, or escalates inappropriately.
- When executed properly, a sur–reply can become the **loudest quiet filing in the entire record.**

- The court's memory is short. The last filing before a ruling often becomes the subconscious map for how the judge understands the dispute.
- Never repeat prior points. Use a sur–reply to *reframe*, *refocus*, and *redirect.*

Core Doctrine

In most litigation, the structure is simple:

- One party files a motion.
- The other replies.
- The original party may submit a reply brief.
- And then, occasionally, the opponent tries to sneak in new material.

That is when the sur–reply becomes not just allowed—but necessary.

A sur–reply is a scalpel, not a mallet. It is used when your opponent goes too far and must be reset.

The sur–reply is not where the argument is made.
It is where the ***narrative is finalized.***

Judges are human.
They often read the last filing first.
They often rule from the impression they most recently digested.
A sharp sur–reply wins not by arguing harder, but by arguing cleaner.

When to Use a Sur–Reply

- Opposing counsel introduces new legal theories not raised in the motion or reply.[22]
- Mischaracterizations of your position are made that, if unaddressed, distort the record.
- The court allows it explicitly, or remains silent long enough that filing one becomes reasonable for record clarity.
- Your opponent uses emotional language, ad hominem, or misinformation that could prejudice a ruling.

What to Include in a Sur–Reply

- **Concise correction of false statements**—not outrage, not rebuttal.
- **Clarification of procedural posture** – remind the court what has and has not been answered.
- **Citations only to the record**—not external authority unless newly introduced by your opponent.
- **Tone: calm, surgical, final.**

Think of it as a judicial alignment tool. Not a counterpunch. A correction.

---

[22] See Fed. R. Civ. P. 7(b) and related practice (courts permit sur-replies when new matters are raised to preserve fairness and completeness of the record); See, e.g., *Khoury v. Meserve*, 268 F. Supp. 2d 600, 605 (D. Md. 2003) (permitting sur-reply when reply raises new arguments)

Universal Application

Most jurisdictions allow a sur–reply only with leave of court. But many courts also permit them when *new matters* are raised in a reply.

Even when not explicitly allowed, a sur–reply can be submitted with the heading:

"Sur–Reply to Clarify Record in Light of Plaintiff's Mischaracterizations"

Or:

"Sur–Reply Filed in Response to New Legal Argument Introduced in Reply Brief"

When written properly, courts rarely reject these. Even if they do not rule on it, they often **read it anyway**—and that is what matters.

Tactical Considerations

Do	Do not
Write short and structured	Argue all over again
Address only new material	Rehash the motion
Use plain language	Use sarcasm or outrage
Submit immediately	Wait and let it rot

Sample Sur–Reply Closers

- *"Respectfully, this filing is limited to correcting one factual and one procedural distortion in Plaintiff's Reply, which if left unaddressed, could prejudice the ruling."*
- *"No new evidence was offered by Plaintiffs. No rebuttal to verified facts was made. Only new legal theories appear, each outside the original motion."*
- *"The record is closed. This sur–reply is submitted not to argue, but to preserve."*

Summary Principles

- **Courts reward clarity.**
- **Final filings matter more than people admit.**
- **Silence after distortion is concession.**
- **The sharpest argument is the last one, if used wisely.**

The Sur–Reply is not about volume.
It is about *resetting the trajectory of the ruling*.
Use it like a lens. Not a club.
And then let the court's memory work in your favor.

Rules of the Doctrine

Rule 1: Correct, Do Not Re-Argue.

A sur–reply exists to correct distortion, not to repeat your brief. You do not restate what is already preserved; you reset what was misrepresented.

Rule 2: Address Only What Is New.
If the opponent introduces no new fact or law, you do not file a sur–reply. Use it only to neutralize additions that threaten to warp the record.

Rule 3: Finalize the Narrative.
The sur–reply is not a counterpunch, it is the last framing. Its purpose is to anchor the judge's subconscious map of the case before decision.

Rule 4: Write Short, Sharp, and Verified.
Brevity is force. A sur–reply should be surgical: numbered, verified, and footnoted only to the record already in evidence.

Rule 5: Preserve Without Emotion.
Tone is everything. Calm precision signals credibility; emotional reply confirms stereotype. The sur–reply must feel inevitable, not reactive.

Rule of War:

The last clean word becomes the court's first remembered truth.

"But sanctify the Lord Christ in your hearts, being ready always to satisfy every one that asketh you a reason of that hope which is in you." (1 Pet. 3:15)

Chapter 20 – Doctrine of Silence

"The Lord will fight for you, and you shall hold your peace." (Exod. 14:14)

BLUF (Bottom Line Up Front):

Silence is not weakness. Silence is a weapon. Properly timed and framed, it denies the enemy information, creates doubt, preserves your record, and magnifies the impact of your words when you finally choose to strike.

Core Doctrine

Silence is not retreat. It is discipline.

Amateurs chatter. Professionals observe.
Opposing counsel wants you to talk too much, too soon, and without discipline. Judges bait you to react emotionally.

Your discipline is silence, until the law and the record demand that you speak. Then, and only then, you strike.

> Example 1: In one trial, saying nothing after the opponent's thirty–minute rant made the judge ask, "Do you wish to respond?" The simple reply—"The

> record reflects my position"—was stronger than any argument.
>
> Example 2: A lawyer once asked three times for a response—silence forced the judge to say, "The objection stands unrebutted."

The court does not measure strength by reply count. It measures posture by clarity and control. If your filings are verified and unrebutted, the law speaks louder than you ever could.

Rules of the Doctrine

Rule 1: Speak Only With Purpose.

Every word must strengthen the record, expose bias, or advance law.

Rule 2: Use Strategic Silence.

Silence unsettles judges and lawyers. It makes them wonder what you know and what you are holding back.

Rule 3: Strike With Timing.

When you do speak, it must feel inevitable—not frantic or reactive.

Rule 4: Control Yourself First.

Emotional silence matters as much as procedural silence. Never scowl, sigh, or show rage.

Rule 5: Break Silence Only for Duty.

If rules are violated—procedure ignored, your right to speak denied, or the record blocked—you must object and preserve. Silence then would be surrender.

Tactical Applications

- **Written Filings.** If it does not advance your theory, preserve the record, or expose bias, do not write it. Save your arrows.
- **Court Hearings.** Speak briefly and formally. Anchor the record, then return to silence.
- **Strategic Silence.** Let opposing counsel over–argue. Let them wonder if you are setting a trap. Doubt creates mistakes.
- **Timed Strikes.** File motions when the opponent is careless, or when the judge is cornered by law. A well–timed filing can derail months of planning.
- **Breaking Silence.**
  – Object if opposing counsel speaks first when you are the moving party.
  – Object if the judge skips pending motions.
  – Object if opposing counsel appears without standing.
  – Object if you are denied the right to preserve the appellate record.

When to Use Strategic Silence

- After filing a verified motion or Judicial Notice that has not been rebutted.
- When opposing counsel replies with rhetoric instead of substance.
- When the court has not ruled and your silence creates procedural pressure.
- When you are ahead and further reply would blur posture instead of clarify it.
- When you expect your opponent to lash out emotionally and want their words to stand alone in the record.

Fail–Safe Tactics

1. **Anchor the Record First.** Never go silent before filing something verified and law–based.
2. **Use Time Intentionally.** Let the docket show clean stretches where only your facts exist.
3. **Preserve Without Filing.** If you are not adding to the record, you are freezing it.
4. **Use Judicial Notice, Not Argument.** If needed, note silence or procedural violation with a short notice rather than a full brief.

Psychological Impact

- Silence forces your opponent to talk to the judge, not to you.
- It reveals desperation. Silence is a mirror—if the other side is unstable, your stillness reflects their collapse.
- Judges notice restraint. Especially when the other side has none.
- In a courtroom full of raised voices, your silence is a signal, an announcement that you will not be baited, rattled, or moved off law.

Why This Works

- Silence denies them information.
- Silence makes your strikes more powerful.
- Silence shields you from traps, while speech—when anchored in law—cuts clean.
- When you speak only with purpose, every word becomes a blade. When you choose silence, every word they speak becomes evidence.
- The disciplined litigant balances both: silence as shield, words as sword.

Rule of War:

Silence is your shield. Speech is your sword. Wield both with precision. Confuse one for the other, and you lose the war.

"But Jesus held his peace." (Matt. 26:63)

Chapter 21 – Doctrine of Adverse Inference

"The wicked man fleeth, when no man pursueth: but the just, bold as a lion, shall be without dread." (Prov. 28:1)

BLUF (Bottom Line Up Front):

When your opponent withholds, destroys, or refuses to produce information, the court can infer that the missing evidence would have harmed their case.
This is the **Doctrine of Adverse Inference** – a tool for turning their silence, obstruction, or avoidance into your advantage.

Key Takeaways

- Courts may draw negative conclusions when a party fails to produce evidence within their control.
- Destruction or concealment of records may support an **adverse inference** that the missing evidence would have been unfavorable.

- This doctrine is **not automatic**—you must frame it precisely, on the record, and often by motion or Judicial Notice.
- Used correctly, adverse inference creates a **procedural shortcut to truth** when full discovery is denied.

Core Doctrine

The Doctrine of Adverse Inference is rooted in simple logic:

"If they had it and it helped them, they would have shown it."

Judges are not allowed to speculate.
But they are permitted—and in some cases required—to draw inferences when one party has exclusive access to evidence and chooses not to present it.

Courts expect parties to protect, disclose, and preserve material evidence.
When that duty is breached, the court may infer that the truth was **too damaging to reveal.**

Universal Basis

The doctrine appears across jurisdictions under different labels:

- **Federal Rule of Civil Procedure 37(e)**: *Failure to preserve ESI may justify adverse inference or default judgment.*

- **Common Law Inference Doctrine**: Courts have long recognized that destruction of evidence creates a **presumption of unfavorable content.**
- **State Civil Codes** (e.g., California, New York, Pennsylvania): Vary by name, but often codify the same logic.

Key case law (widely cited):

- ***Zubulake v. UBS Warburg LLC***, 229 F.R.D. 422, 430 (S.D.N.Y. 2004) (failure to preserve evidence supports adverse inference)
- ***Leon v. IDX Systems Corp.***, 541 F.3d 903, 911 (9th Cir. 2008) (upholding adverse inference and sanctions for spoliation of electronic evidence)
- ***Schmid v. Milwaukee Electric Tool Corp.***, 13 F.3d 76, 79 (3d Cir. 1994) (establishing factors governing sanctions and adverse inference for destruction of evidence)

Rules of the Doctrine

Rule 1: Name the absence, and you define the truth the court may infer.

Unspoken gaps become speculation; articulated gaps become evidence.

Rule 2: Silence over controlled evidence is not neutral.

When a party alone holds the record and refuses to reveal it, the law permits the court to infer that the truth harms them.

Rule 3: Frame each omission as a decision, not an accident.
Adverse inference attaches only when the court sees intent or indifference—not mere loss.

Rule 4: Give the court the logic it cannot state on its own.

Judges cannot speculate, but they can adopt the inference you build on the record.

Rule 5: Let their disappearance speak louder than your argument.

Missing evidence, when properly framed, becomes testimony they cannot rebut.

How to Trigger an Adverse Inference

1. **Establish Control**
   Show the opposing party had possession or control of the document, file, or record.
2. **Establish Relevance**
   Argue that the withheld material is directly related to a claim or defense.
3. **Establish Absence or Destruction**
   Identify that the material was never produced, or was destroyed, redacted, or inexplicably lost.

4. **Establish Notice or Duty**
   Show that the party knew—or should have known—the material was relevant and subject to preservation.
5. **Request Adverse Inference by Motion or Judicial Notice**
   The court will not infer on its own. You must request it directly and clearly.

Situational Triggers

Situation	Adverse Inference Signal
Server logs deleted after litigation begins	Data likely shows fault or suppression
Courtroom audio altered or transcript backdated	True record contradicts court's narrative
Key witnesses are withheld or suddenly unavailable	Testimony would harm opponent's case
Opponent invokes broad privilege with no explanation	Documents likely reveal misconduct or contradiction
Filing deadlines are missed without explanation	Party lacks factual support to respond

---

Filing Language to Use

- *"Plaintiff's failure to produce the requested records, which were under their exclusive control, creates a strong presumption that the contents would be unfavorable to their position."*

- *"Defendant's failure to provide the original server logs, coupled with their assertion of privilege without specificity, supports an adverse inference of concealment."*
- *"Where relevant evidence is withheld without cause, the court is permitted to infer that its production would have harmed the party that failed to present it."*

Strategic Use

Adverse inference is especially powerful when:

- Your opponent is procedurally aggressive but substantively evasive.
- The court is reluctant to sanction, but open to soft corrections.
- The absence of data can be ***made louder than the data itself.***

Used wisely, this doctrine lets you *win the point without proving the content*—by shifting the burden to your opponent's silence.

Summary Principles

- **Do not let missing evidence go unspoken. Name the absence.**
- **Let the court draw the inference—but give it the scaffolding.**
- **Frame each omission as a decision—because it is.**

The court cannot admit speculation.
But it can accept logic.
And logic says:
"If they had it and it helped them, they would have used it."

Rule of War

Name what they hide, and the court will see what they fear.

"For there is nothing hid, which shall not be made manifest." (Mark 4:22)

Chapter 22 – Doctrine of the Litigation Hold

Truth must be preserved before it can be revealed.

"Bind up the testimony,
seal the law among my disciples."
– Isaiah 8:16

BLUF (Bottom Line Up Front)

A litigation hold is your first strike in the war for evidence—the moment you shift the burden onto your opponent so that any data loss becomes *their* problem, not yours.

From the instant litigation is reasonably anticipated, every party—including government actors—has a non-discretionary duty to prescrve all documents, metadata, audio, video, emails, logs, drafts, and records relevant to the dispute.

Failure to impose a litigation hold is not a mistake; it is a breach of duty and often the first step in spoliation.

A proper litigation hold freezes the battlefield. It prevents destruction, forces adversaries into compliance, and positions you to win adverse inference or sanctions if destruction occurs anyway.

A Pro Se litigant who knows how to impose, document, and weaponize a litigation hold becomes immune to the most common tactic of corrupt institutions: **destroying the truth before the fight begins.**

The Doctrine

Litigation is not merely argument.
It is evidence—preserved, produced, analyzed, and weaponized.

And evidence exists long before motions do.

The legal system recognizes this.
That is why, the moment litigation becomes "reasonably foreseeable," every party has a **legal duty to preserve** all potentially relevant evidence.[23]

This duty arises **before filing**, **before service**, **before the first motion**, even before the first Judicial Notice.

It applies to:

- private parties,
- corporations,
- state agencies,
- counties,
- clerks,
- judges' chambers,
- law firms,

---

[23] See *Zubulake v. UBS Warburg LLC*, 220 F.R.D. 212, 218 (S.D.N.Y. 2003) (duty to preserve arises when litigation is reasonably anticipated)

- and every employee with access to records.

Yet litigation holds are almost never discussed in Pro Se contexts —
because the legal guild hopes you never learn how decisive they are.

The Purpose of a Litigation Hold

A litigation hold functions as:

- a **freeze order**,
- a **warning shot**,
- a **procedural trap**,
- an **evidentiary insurance policy**,
- and the **foundation** for spoliation sanctions later.

When you send a litigation hold letter:

1. **You define the universe of evidence.**
2. **You trigger the opponent's legal duty to preserve.**
3. **You create a paper trail proving they knew of that duty.**
4. **You position yourself to win sanctions automatically when they destroy anything.**

Lawyers fear litigation holds because once a hold is issued, **every deletion is a confession.**

And corrupt institutions fear them because a properly documented hold exposes:

- altered transcripts,
- missing logs,
- overwritten metadata,
- "lost" emails,
- destroyed ballot images,
- missing CCTV,
- curated case files,
- and everything they hoped would never see the record.

A litigation hold is a boundary:
Cross it, and the law punishes the destroyer.

Rules of the Doctrine

Rule 1: The duty to preserve begins before the case begins.

Once litigation is reasonably foreseeable, every party must freeze evidence.
Ignorance is not a defense.

Rule 2: A litigation hold must be explicit, written, and documented.

If it is not in writing, it does not exist.
If it is not served, it cannot be enforced.

Rule 3: Failure to implement a litigation hold may constitute spoliation depending on the circumstances and resulting loss of evidence.

You do not need to prove intentional deletion to trigger the spoliation chain; failure to preserve after notice can be enough to shift the burden and support sanctions.

Rule 4: Your litigation hold is a trap, not a suggestion.

Once served, every missing document becomes presumptively harmful to the opponent.

Rule 5: Litigation hold letters protect you and expose them.

You preserve your own evidence; you trap them in their own misconduct.

Rule 6: Silence after a litigation hold is admission.

If they do not acknowledge the hold, the court presumes they ignored it.

Rule 7: A litigation hold is the first step in the spoliation chain.

Hold → Destruction → Inference → Sanction → Victory
This doctrine weaponizes that sequence.

Tactical Applications

1. Issue Litigation Hold Immediately

Send a **Litigation Hold Notice** as soon as a dispute arises—not after filing.
Send it via:

- certified mail
- email with read-receipt
- hand-delivery (if necessary)

Document all service.

---

2. Define the Evidence Universe Broadly

List categories:

- emails, logs, text messages
- drafts, internal notes
- audio, video, CCTV
- metadata, PDFs, revisions
- transcripts, clerk messages
- ballot images, chain-of-custody
- server records

Broad categories force broad preservation.

3. Demand Suspension of Auto-Delete Policies

Most spoliation comes from "routine deletion."
Your hold letter forces them to disable automatic purges.

---

4. Require Preservation of Metadata

Without metadata, a PDF is meaningless.
Litigation holds must expressly state:

"Preserve original metadata, including creation/modification timestamps, hash values, audit logs, and revision history."

This single sentence wins cases.

---

5. Judicial Notice the Litigation Hold

File a **Judicial Notice of Litigation Hold Served on [Date]**.
This locks the duty into the court record and traps them the moment they destroy anything.

Once this is filed, every act of deletion becomes:

- spoliation,
- sanctionable,
- appealable,
- and a procedural confession.

Rule of War

He who preserves the battlefield controls the battle. Freeze the evidence early, and every destruction becomes your proof.

"Hold fast that which is good."
— 1 Thessalonians 5:21

(Preserve the truth, and the truth will preserve you.)

Chapter 23 – Doctrine of Spoliation

When Destruction Becomes Confession

"The wicked man shall be taken away by his own iniquity: and he shall fall by his own sin."
— Proverbs 5:22
(The hand that destroys evidence destroys its own defense.)

BLUF (Bottom Line Up Front):

Spoliation is not mere misconduct—it is *a legal admission disguised as destruction.*
When your opponent destroys, alters, conceals, withholds, or fabricates evidence, the law gives you the strongest remedy in civil procedure: **the presumption that the missing evidence supports an inference that the truth would have been unfavorable to the party who failed to produce it.**

Spoliation flips the battlefield.
What they hoped to erase becomes the very proof they feared.

Properly captured and documented, spoliation turns every act of destruction into an uncontested fact, an adverse inference, or a basis for sanctions up to **default judgment, fee-shifting, and contempt**.

Spoliation is not a setback.
Spoliation is victory delivered by your opponent's own hand.[24]

The Doctrine

Every system actor who fears truth eventually destroys it.
Evidence goes "missing."
Transcripts appear "corrected."
Emails fail to "archive properly."
Metadata "accidentally overwrites."
Audio "cannot be located."
Government logs "auto-delete."

These are not coincidences.
They are confessions—silent, involuntary, and devastating.

Spoliation doctrine turns intentional or negligent destruction into proof of guilt.
Under federal and state law:

- **If they had the evidence and destroyed it → the court may infer the evidence would have been unfavorable.**

This is not rhetoric.
It is black-letter law.

---

[24] ***Fed. R. Civ. P. 37(e)*** (authorizing sanctions for failure to preserve electronically stored information)

Three Levels of Spoliation (All Weaponized in PSLW)

1. **Failure to Preserve**
   They knew litigation was pending and still allowed evidence to be lost.

2. **Destruction or Alteration**
   Logs wiped, transcripts curated, metadata overwritten, ballots shredded, emails deleted.

3. **Fabrication or Substitution**
   The most damning form—false versions, edited transcripts, backdated PDFs, reconstructed "copies."

Spoliation is not about motive.
It is about **duty + destruction = presumption**.

Once shown, the burden shifts onto *them*—they must explain the missing evidence. Almost no one can.

Rules of the Doctrine

Rule 1: Spoliation is an admission, not an accident.

What they destroy becomes proof of what they feared.

Rule 2: The duty to preserve begins the moment litigation is imminent.

Emails, logs, video, transcripts, chain-of-custody files, server data—all must be preserved.
If not, they have already confessed.

Rule 3: Absence + Relevance = Adverse Inference as a matter of law.

The missing item is presumed harmful to the destroyer unless they *prove otherwise.*

Rule 4: Spoliation escalates sanction levels.

Minor: evidentiary inference
Moderate: fees, costs, preclusion
Severe: issue sanctions, striking pleadings
Terminal: **default judgment** or **dismissal with prejudice**

Rule 5: You do not accuse—you document.

You file:

- Verified Judicial Notice of Spoliation
- Exhibit Summary with timestamps / metadata
- Adverse Inference Motion under controlling rule
- Proposed Order imposing presumption

The record, not your emotion, convicts them.

Rule 6: Sanctions and inferences are discretionary, but structured absence narrows that discretion.

Courts may impose adverse inference, evidentiary sanctions, or default remedies depending on the severity of the loss and the degree of fault.

Your task is to eliminate ambiguity so the court's discretion collapses toward a single lawful outcome.

Tactical Applications

1. When evidence "goes missing," you frame the loss, not the motive.

Use language like:

- "The evidence was within opposing counsel's exclusive control."
- "Its absence materially prejudices Defendant."
- "Spoliation inference is appropriate."

Do *not* say "corrupt" or "fraudulent."
Say "spoliation," "variance," "loss," "absence," "failure to preserve."

---

2. Use Visual Law to expose the destruction.

A simple table wins:

Evidence	Required Action	What Happened	Governing Law	Adverse Inference

One table → five seconds → sanction.

---

3. Metadata is your nuclear proof.

When transcripts are altered, emails changed, PDFs recreated:

- Check PDF creation date
- Check audio file duration
- Check hash values
- Check EXIF data
- Compare "modified" vs. "created" timestamps

A single mismatched timestamp is a spoliation confession.

---

4. Destroyed evidence justifies default judgment.

Under *Rule 37(e)*, *Rule 4011*, and common law principles:[25]

If they destroyed central evidence *after litigation began*, you move for:

- **Issue sanctions**

---

[25] *Celotex Corp. v. Catrett*, 477 U.S. 317, 322–23 (1986)

- **Preclusion**
- **Facts deemed admitted**
- **Default judgment on liability**

Most lawyers fear default more than losing the case—because default is unspinnable.

---

5. Spoliation is your appellate parachute.

Appeals reverse when:

- The trial court failed to sanction destruction
- The evidence was uniquely within the opponent's control
- The Pro Se litigant preserved the issue cleanly

Appellate judges recoil from spoliation.
It is the one misconduct they cannot excuse.

Rule of War:

When they destroy evidence, they destroy themselves. Document the loss, invoke the law, and let their silence confess the truth.

"For nothing is hidden that shall not be made manifest; nor secret that shall not be known and come to light."
— Luke 8:17

Chapter 24 – Doctrine of the Audible Record

"Write this for a memorial in a book, and deliver it to the ears of Josue." (Exod. 17:14)

BLUF (Bottom Line Up Front):

In many courtrooms, **the written transcript is not the whole truth**.
Clerks, stenographers, or judicial staff may omit, reframe, or backdate transcripts—intentionally or through error.
The **Audible Record Doctrine** is the strategic use of certified courtroom audio to expose contradiction, correct falsification, and re–anchor the legal record in **verifiable reality**.

Key Takeaways

- The **courtroom audio file** is often more complete—and more dangerous to manipulation—than the official transcript.
- Most litigants forget it exists. Most lawyers do not request it. That is a mistake.

- Audio can be used to **identify contradictions**, **prove tampering**, and **restore what written records try to erase**.
- Weaponizing the audible record requires process, patience, and proper authentication.

Core Doctrine

The truth is not always what is written.
It is what was said.

Judges and clerks may delay issuing transcripts for weeks or months.
When they arrive, they may omit sidebars, off–the–record comments, statements made before official start times, or language damaging to the court's posture.

This is not theory. It happens.
And when it does, **the audio file becomes the fallback truth.**

The Audible Record Doctrine treats courtroom audio as ***an independent evidentiary layer***—one that can be:

- Transcribed unofficially
- Time–stamped
- Compared to the certified transcript
- Submitted to force Judicial Notice of the gap

Rules of the Doctrine

Rule 1: Trust the audio before you trust the transcript.

What is spoken is truth; what is typed may be curated.

Rule 2: Treat every hearing as a recoverable waveform.

If the transcript later contradicts the audio, the audio governs.[26]

Rule 3: Preserve the chain of custody before the story changes.

Metadata, timestamps, and download logs become your shield against manipulation.

Rule 4: Expose variance, not motive.

Courts correct contradictions when shown the gap—without being forced to admit why it exists.

Rule 5: Let the tape speak where argument cannot.

The audible record carries a credibility no brief can match; use it to anchor the truth.

How to Execute the Doctrine

1. **Request the Audio**

---

[26] ***Fed. R. App. P. 10(c)*** (permitting reconstruction or correction of the record when transcript is incomplete or inaccurate)

    - File a formal request to obtain the full audio record under local or statewide rules.
    - Do this **before** the official transcript is released.
2. **Preserve Chain of Custody**
    - Retain all metadata. Time of creation, file size, download logs.
    - Document when it was received and by whom.
3. **Compare and Annotate**
    - Use software or a human transcript tool to build an unofficial transcript.
    - Highlight any **omissions, errors, contradictions, or backdated phrasing**.
4. **File a Judicial Notice**
    - Include:
        - The official transcript
        - Your unofficial annotated version
        - The original audio file (on disc or online storage)
    - Notify the court that **a variance exists** and must be resolved before ruling.
5. **Propose Resolution**
    - Ask for:
        - Transcript correction

- Supplemental testimony acknowledgment
- Evidentiary status of the omitted sections

Tactical Triggers for the Doctrine

Trigger	Inference
Court delays transcript for weeks	Potential editing or curation
Transcript excludes pre–hearing sidebar	Record is sanitized
Judge denies or misstates something you recall clearly	Opportunity to submit contradiction via audio
Ruling contradicts verbal on–the–record statements	Audio can undermine legitimacy or create appeal ground

---

Legal Leverage

- **Federal Rule of Appellate Procedure 10(c)**: Appellants may prepare their own transcript when one is unavailable or inadequate.
- **18 U.S.C. § 1512(c)**: Alteration or destruction of court records is a federal crime if done to obstruct.
- **Common Law Preservation Principle**: The court cannot ignore material discrepancies once made part of the record.

Language to Use in Filing

- *"The official transcript, as issued, omits language that is present in the certified courtroom audio. This variance is material to the case and must be reconciled."*
- *"Attached is a certified audio file, its playback timeline, and an annotated unofficial transcript highlighting missing or contradictory statements."*
- *"This Notice is not an objection. It is a preservation mechanism for appellate and federal oversight of the case record."*

Why This Works

- Audio is hard to fake.
- Transcripts are often generated weeks later—making manipulation easier.
- Courts cannot un–hear what was said.
- When caught in contradiction, courts often **correct transcripts quietly**, rather than risk public exposure.

Summary Principles

- The written record is not the only record.
- If the transcript contradicts memory, **verify the waveform**.

- Courts rely on trust. When the audible record breaks that trust, **control shifts to the party who preserved the truth.**

The Audible Record Doctrine does not argue.
It plays the tape.
And when truth is spoken—even once—it echoes louder than any ruling.

Rule of War

When the transcript lies, play the tape. The tape never lies.

"Faith then cometh by hearing; and hearing by the word of Christ." (Rom. 10:17)

Chapter 25 – Doctrine Triad I—Velocity · Attrition · Minimalism

---

Velocity (Decisive Action)

"The hand of the diligent shall rule: but that which is slothful shall be under tribute."
— Proverbs 12:24
(Act first, rule the field.)

Attrition (Endurance and Faith)

"He that shall persevere to the end, shall be saved."
— Daniel 12:13 (LXX reading parallel)
(Persistence is deliverance.)

Minimalism (Restraint and Wisdom)

"He that spareth his words is learned: and a man of understanding is of a precious spirit."
— Proverbs 17:27
(Measured speech is strength.)

BLUF (Bottom Line Up Front):

Winning is not loyalty to one mode—it is choosing the correct mode at the correct time. Learn the three operational postures, then switch fast.

Mastery is not strength in one posture, but precision in all three.

Rules of the Doctrine (Triad I)

Rule 1: Velocity wins the moment; attrition wins the war; minimalism wins the record.

Each posture creates a different kind of dominance.

Rule 2: Choose the mode the situation demands—not the mode your emotions prefer.

Strategy beats instinct.

Rule 3: Velocity opens the field, attrition shapes it, minimalism seals it.

Use each posture for its intended role.

Rule 4: Switch modes fast—fixed posture is defeat.

Rigidity is predictable; adaptability is victory.

---

1. Velocity (Shock)

When: Emergencies, injunction windows, ex parte opportunity, or when you must seize narrative control.
How: Rapid, narrow filings that create facts on the docket

before the opponent can reply. Use certified service, time-stamped exhibits, and short, commanding orders.
Effect: Forces opponents and court into reaction; sets the initial frame.
Rule of War: Strike first, strike clean—momentum begets leverage.

---

2. Attrition (Siege)

When: Long fights, resource asymmetry, or when adversary relies on delay.
How: Relentless preservation—document every issue, object methodically, appeal when structure is violated, and keep the record air-tight. Log hours, costs, and abuses.
Effect: Converts endurance into leverage; attrition breaks teams and budgets.
Rule of War: Outlast; the system favors those who quit.

---

3. Procedural Minimalism (Sniper)

When: Court or counsel brands you "vexatious" or when every filing risks being dismissed as noise.
How: One surgical filing: verified, perfectly sourced, and appellate-ready. File it, then go silent. Let the record speak.
Effect: Restores credibility; magnifies the power of a single correct entry.
Rule of War: Precision amplifies influence; restraint sharpens the record.

When to Shift—a One–Line Decision Matrix

- If deadlines demand presence → **Velocity**.
- If opponent bets on time or money → **Attrition**.
- If reputation is the obstacle → **Minimalism**.

(If two conditions coincide, pair modes: velocity to secure an immediate posture, then attrition to sustain—minimalism for cleanup and appeal.)

Quick Reference (for filings)

- **Velocity filing:** 1–2 pages + proposed order + stamped exhibit; certified service.
- **Attrition filing:** documented timeline + verification table + cost log.
- **Minimalism filing:** single issue, verified affidavit, one proposed remedial order, appellate hook.

Rule of War (Triad I):

Strike fast when the window is thin.
Grind when time favors you.
Stay silent and surgical when reputation must be repaired.

Velocity (Immediate Obedience)

"Whatsoever thy hand is able to do, do it earnestly."
— Ecclesiasticus 9:10
(Swift action in righteousness.)

Attrition (Perseverance under Trial)

"Let us not be weary in doing good: for in due time we shall reap, not failing."
— Galatians 6:9
(Endure; the harvest comes.)

Minimalism (Quiet Strength)

"Let your speech be yea, yea: no, no: and that which is over and above these, is of evil."
— Matthew 5:37
(Truth needs no surplus words.)

"Let all things be done decently, and according to order."—1 Cor. 14:40
(Discernment governs all action.)

Chapter 26 – Doctrine of Velocity

"Make haste to help me, O Lord, my salvation." (Ps. 38:22)

BLUF (Bottom Line Up Front):

Litigation is not just about substance. It is also about timing. This is the controlled use of filing momentum to shape perception, control court cadence, and exhaust opponent resources—while **preserving your own energy and clarity**.

Key Takeaways

- Momentum matters. The side that moves with rhythm, not panic, often controls the outcome.
- Too many filings too fast creates confusion. Too few creates doubt. The correct pace is ***as needed, not as possible***.
- Velocity is not volume. It is **sequenced precision.**
- The opponent must always feel pressure. The court must never feel chaos.

Core Doctrine

The most powerful filings are not just well–written—they are ***well–timed.***

Each motion, reply, or notice must serve a purpose:

- To establish posture,
- To cut off ambiguity,
- To frame the record,
- Or to respond to distortion.

Velocity is the art of **hitting when it counts, not when it is expected.**

The court reads rhythm.
The opponent reads pressure.
Momentum decides perception.

Example 1: Filing a verified notice within twelve hours of a distorted order changed the tempo—the opponent was suddenly reacting, not leading.

Example 2: In another case, spacing filings by a full week created contrast: the opponent flooded the docket daily, while the Pro Se record looked calm and deliberate.

Rules of the Doctrine

Rule 1: Velocity is not speed—it is timing.

A filing lands hardest when it arrives at the moment the system is unprepared.

Rule 2: File only with purpose, never with panic.

Momentum is control; haste is confusion. Courts can tell the difference instantly.

Rule 3: Anchoring rhythm shapes perception.

A timely motion frames the case; a timely silence sharpens it.

Rule 4: Let the opponent race while you decide.

Velocity is not matching their chaos—it is making them chase your order.

Rule 5: Strike only when the record changes, not when your emotions change.

Impact comes from precision, not frequency.

Three Modes of Velocity

Mode	Description	Purpose
Anchor Mode	A series of filings (motion + notice + proposed order) to frame the case	Controls narrative and posture
Pulse Mode	Single, clean filings spaced intentionally to avoid court fatigue	Preserves clarity, avoids judicial annoyance

Mode	Description	Purpose
Overrun Mode	Used only to force decision or punish delay. Fast, sharp filings to overwhelm obstruction.	Used when opponent or court stalls

---

When to Accelerate

- Opponent files without rebutting fact
- Court delays a dispositive ruling unreasonably
- False statements are left unanswered
- Trial posture is assumed without a ruling

Each acceleration must include:

- A clear purpose
- An endpoint
- And ***no emotional overreach***

Velocity is measured by impact, not output.

When to Pause

- Your last filing was clean, unrebutted, and verified
- Opponent has overfiled and appears desperate
- Court has indicated motion review is pending

- Momentum is in your favor and additional filings would dilute clarity

Do not overfile.
Let the court fill the silence.
Let the opponent flood the docket and reveal their panic.

Never break your own signal with noise.

Language and Framing

- *"This Motion is filed to preserve procedural clarity in light of the opponent's inconsistent posture."*
- *"Filed now to ensure the record reflects unbroken notice of unrebutted material fact."*
- *"No further filings will be made unless the court or opponent reopens ambiguity."*

Summary Principles

- Litigation moves in tempo.
  Those who master rhythm, master control.
- Velocity is not filing speed—it is **strategic weight delivered at the right moment.**
- File with impact. Pause with intention. Respond with precision.

The best motion is not just what you file.
It is **when you file it.**
And it is *the silence you choose not to break.*

Rule of War

Hit the docket at the moment of maximum consequence—timing is the strike.

"And immediately, leaving their nets, they followed him." (Matt. 4:20)

Chapter 27 – Doctrine of Attrition

"The just shall live in his faith." (Hab. 2:4)

BLUF (Bottom Line Up Front):

Most institutions do not win cases. They wait out their opponents.
The **Attrition Doctrine** reverses that paradigm: it is the deliberate use of procedural stamina, reputational cost–shifting, and time asymmetry to force institutions—government actors, courts, or firms—to abandon weak cases they can no longer justify continuing.

Key Takeaways

- Attrition is not delay. It is **targeted endurance.**
- Law firms and public entities have limits: political, reputational, and financial.
- Pro Se litigants are not bound by billing, internal approval, or PR cycles.

- When executed correctly, the Attrition Doctrine forces the opposition to bleed resources into a case **they no longer want to carry.**

Core Doctrine

The legal system favors the persistent—not the loud.
Government lawyers do not like fighting uphill.
Law firms do not like dragging out cases that produce losses or public embarrassment.
Judges do not like managing dockets that will not go away and threaten appellate exposure.

The Attrition Doctrine treats the litigation process like a **slow pressure chamber**:

- No escalation unless necessary
- No settlement unless advantageous
- No withdrawal unless it comes from them

You do not outfight the system.
You **outlast** it—cleanly, procedurally, and visibly.

Example 1: After years of filings, a county solicitor privately told his client the case had to end—not because they lost on law, but because they could no longer justify the reputational cost of continuing.

Example 2: A firm billed hundreds of hours to fight a 3-page verified motion; the cost alone pushed their client toward settlement.

Example 3: In one case, the judge openly asked opposing counsel, "Why are we still here?"—attrition had shifted the pressure to the court itself.

Rules of the Doctrine

Rule 1: Attrition is not delay—it is controlled endurance.

You do not stall the case; you shape it through disciplined persistence.

Rule 2: Every filing you make must cost them more than it costs you.

Asymmetric pressure breaks institutions long before it breaks you.

Rule 3: Silence is part of the siege.

When the record is clean, let your opponent exhaust themselves trying to fill the void.

Rule 4: Outlast with structure, not emotion.

Endurance wins only when it is procedural, verified, and visible to the court.

Rule 5: Leave the opposition an exit that looks like their idea.

Institutional actors retreat faster when they can save face.

How to Execute the Doctrine

1. **Preserve Your Energy**
    - File only when strategically required.
    - Let the court and your opponent overextend.
2. **Impose Asymmetric Costs**
    - Each of your filings costs them 10x in review, drafting, partner time, or client risk.
    - Their fear of discovery, exposure, or media coverage is often stronger than their belief in the case.
3. **Leave the Door Open for Retreat**
    - Offer the court a graceful exit.
    - Let opposing counsel blame the withdrawal on "resource balancing," not your superiority.
    - That preserves your victory and their narrative collapse.

Tactical Triggers

Opponent Behavior	Attrition Response
Excessive filings	File once. Let them flood the docket.
Falsehoods or distortions	Respond only to factual points. Preserve silence otherwise.

Opponent Behavior	Attrition Response
Delay tactics	File a preservation notice, then wait.
Summary judgment avoidance	Trigger Rule 1035.3(d) or equivalent, and stop filing. Let the record tighten.

Summary Principles

- Persistence is a tactic. But structured persistence becomes a weapon.
- Law firms crack under cost.
- Governments crack under exposure.
- Courts crack under weight.

The winner is not always the last to fight.
It is the one who kept filing long after the other side forgot why they started.

Rule of War

Endure longer than they can justify—and the system will fold first.

"But he that shall persevere to the end, he shall be saved." (Matt. 24:13)

Chapter 28 – Doctrine of Procedural Minimalism

"In much speaking thou shalt not want sin: but he that refraineth his lips is most wise." (Prov. 10:19)

BLUF (Bottom Line Up Front):

Not every battle requires fire. Judges and lawyers expect Pro Se litigants to drown the docket with noise. Procedural Minimalism means filing only what is necessary, at the sharpest possible moment, and letting silence or the record itself do the rest. Less paper, more precision.

Why Minimalism Matters

- **Perception Bias:** Courts stereotype Pro Se as filing too much—"paper terrorists" or "vexatious litigants."
- **Weaponized Silence:** Sometimes the strongest filing is *no filing at all*—forcing your opponent or the judge to sit in their own error.

- **Appellate Leverage:** Appellate courts respect brevity. The cleaner the record, the harder it is to dismiss you as unfocused.
- **Strategic Timing:** Flooding early can burn credibility; holding back creates pressure.

The Balance of Minimalism and Velocity

- *Velocity Doctrine:* File rapidly to overwhelm when urgency demands.
- *Procedural Minimalism Doctrine:* File sparingly to show discipline and let the opposition overplay their hand.
- **Together:** Like a sniper and a machine gun—each has its place. The master knows which to use.

Rules of Doctrine

Rule 1: File only when it moves the needle.

If it does not force a ruling, preserve a right, or build the appeal, it is noise.

Rule 2: One clean strike beats ten weak ones.

Precision filings carry weight; clutter carries risk.

Rule 3: Preserve without noise.

A single Judicial Notice can anchor the record more strongly than a stack of motions.

Rule 4: Let silence speak before you do.

When the court ignores your motion, wait—then file a Notice of Constructive Denial.

Rule 5: Write for the appeal, not the room.

A minimalist record is easier to defend and harder to dismiss.

Tactical Applications

- **Judge taunts you in court:** Do not argue. File *one* Judicial Notice of Transcript Variance—short, verified, clinical.
- **Opposing counsel lies repeatedly:** File *one* Motion for Sanctions citing Pa.R.C.P. 1023.1, attach exhibits. Let them respond 20 pages—you have already won the contrast.
- **Court suppresses filings:** Instead of five angry notices, file *one* Judicial Notice with timestamped confirmation logs. Clean, deadly.
- **Appellate brief:** Do not re–argue everything. Pick 2–3 strongest preserved issues. A minimalist brief with record citations often beats a sprawling rant.

Why This Works

- **It flips the stereotype.** Judges expect clutter. You give clarity. They cannot dismiss you as "vexatious."

- **It magnifies impact.** When you file less, every motion carries more weight.
- **It saves endurance.** Litigation is attrition. Minimalism conserves your energy while draining theirs.
- **It strengthens appeal.** A lean, precise record is a weapon appellate judges respect—and AI systems in the future will reward.

Rule of War:

Do not fire every shot. Procedural Minimalism is knowing that sometimes the most powerful move is restraint. One precise strike, one clean record, one appellate hook—that is enough to kill a case.

"But let your speech be yea, yea: no, no." (Matt. 5:37)

Chapter 29—Doctrine of Veracity, Verification, and Sanctions

"Lying lips are an abomination to the Lord: but they that deal faithfully are his delight."
— Proverbs 12:22

BLUF (Bottom Line Up Front):

A lawyer who knowingly misstates law or fact does not err—he corrupts the record.
Verification strips away the presumption of candor; sanctions impose the cost.
Always verify. Always demand sanctions. Silence means adoption; sanctions mean deterrence.

The Doctrine

The justice system assumes lawyers tell the truth.
When that assumption is abused, the lie becomes precedent.
A verified Pro Se record collapses the fiction—but exposure alone is not enough.
Fraud must be punished, or it repeats.

Three Pillars

1. **Veracity**—Treat every unverified claim as conjecture.
2. **Verification**—Sworn, evidenced, exhibit-tagged filings define the record.
3. **Sanctions**—Quantify harm and demand payment sufficient to deter and punish.

When counsel's words are proven false on a verified record, the court not only may—but must—sanction under rule, statute, or inherent power.[27]

Rules of the Doctrine

Rule 1: Treat every unverified assertion as conjecture.

If it is not sworn, sourced, or cited, it is noise.

Rule 2: Verification is your armor.

Sworn, evidenced filings redefine the record in your terms, not theirs.

Rule 3: Document the lie before you name it.

A simple table—quote, claimed cite, actual source, impact—turns emotion into evidence.

Rule 4: Expose and punish in the same filing cycle.

[27] *Chambers v. NASCO, Inc.*, 501 U.S. 32, 44–45 (1991) (courts possess inherent authority to sanction bad-faith conduct)

A sanctions demand gains power when paired with verified contradiction.

Rule 5: Quantify the sanction with method, not outrage.

Courts respect numbers they can audit—and distrust emotions they cannot.

Rule 6: Seek layered remedies.

Money for harm, referral for discipline, and findings for the appellate record.

Rule 7: Maintain professional diction while documenting fraud.

Use "misrepresentation," "lack of candor," "fraud upon the tribunal." Precision protects you.

Sanction Formula (for Pro Se Use)

> **Total Sanction = Documented Time Value + Direct Costs + Deterrent Multiplier (× 2 – 3) + Punitive Component for Egregious Conduct.**
>
> **a. Documented Time Value** – Log hours × prevailing local attorney or paralegal rate. Attach affidavit.
> **b. Direct Costs** – Filing, copies, transcripts, postage, travel, experts.
> **c. Deterrent Multiplier** – × 2 for knowing lies; × 3 for systemic or strategic deceit.
> **d. Punitive Component** – Add a fixed figure (e.g.,

$10 000–$25 000) when the fraud inflicted reputational or procedural harm. Cite *Chambers v. NASCO*, 501 U.S. 32 (1991).
e. State the math on record. Courts respect numbers they can audit.

Sample language

*"Defendant requests sanctions of (A) documented time value $, **(B) verified costs $**, multiplied by two for deterrence = $, **plus a punitive sanction of $** to compensate harm and deter recurrence."*

Tactical Applications

1. **Verification Table**
    - A 1-page exhibit with four columns:
      A Quoted text • **B** Claimed citation • **C** Actual source or "none" • **D** Case impact.
    - Attach screenshots or certified copies.
2. **Verified Sur-Reply with Sanctions Demand**
    - Short, factual, numbered. Include: verification affidavit + table + cost affidavit.
3. **Safe-Harbor Compliance**
    - If local rule (e.g., FRCP 11) requires notice, send certified demand letter; file after lapse.
4. **Preserve for Appeal & Discipline**

- Obtain written finding: “The Court finds counsel knowingly misrepresented X.” That phrase is gold on appeal.

5. **Referral & Public Record**
    - When deceit is intentional, request referral to the bar and prosecutor.
    - Publicize only after order is final.

Evidence Checklist

☑ Verified affidavit (28 U.S.C. § 1746 or state equivalent)
☑ Verification Table with sources
☑ Fee or time log affidavit
☑ Screenshots / certified authority copies
☑ Safe-harbor letter (if applicable)

Common Pushbacks & Responses

- **“It was a mistake.”** Demand verified retraction and fees.
- **“Safe harbor not observed.”** Show proof or explain exigency.
- **“Sanctions chill advocacy.”** Truth is not chilled by accountability.

Rule of War:

Verify the truth, expose the lie, and make the sanction the lesson.

"Be not deceived, God is not mocked. For what things a man shall sow, those also shall he reap." (Galatians 6:7)

Chapter 30 – Doctrine of the Legal Incantation

"A fool's mouth is his destruction: and his lips are the ruin of his soul."
— Proverbs 18:7

BLUF (Bottom Line Up Front):

Words without evidence are noise.
When counsel hides behind legal jargon—calling verified fact "frivolous," "vexatious," or "conjecture"—he admits he cannot refute it.
A legal incantation is not a response; it is an admission of no proof.

Incantations collapse when unsupported by record or law.

The Doctrine

The modern courtroom speaks two languages: law and theater.
Theater begins when an attorney substitutes labels for proof—reciting *frivolous*, *irrelevant*, or *without merit* instead of addressing documents, exhibits, or law.
These phrases are not argument; they are rhetorical smoke

grenades.

Under the Rules of Civil Procedure, a statement without evidentiary support is a *bald assertion* and carries no legal weight. Under **Pa.R.C.P. 1029(b)** and ***Bundy v. Dep't of Corr.***, 243 A.3d 19, 35–36 (Pa. 2020), silence, denial without record support, or conclusory adjectives are admissions by operation of law.

Every time counsel answers verified fact with terminology instead of substance, he commits a silent confession—and, when repeated, sanctionable bad faith.

Rules of the Doctrine

Rule 1: Name the incantation the moment it appears.

A label without evidence is not argument—it is a confession of insufficiency.

Rule 2: Demand proof or withdrawal for every adjective used as law.

If counsel cannot cite the record, the incantation collapses into admission under Rule 1029(b).

Rule 3: Quote the controlling rule, not their rhetoric.

"Averments not specifically denied are admitted." Let the rule translate their silence into truth.

Rule 4: Translate every insult into its real meaning.

"Frivolous" means they cannot rebut the fact. "Vexatious" means your filings are working. "Conjecture" means you have evidence they fear.

Rule 5: Treat repetition as bad faith, not style.

One incantation is desperation. Repeated incantations are sanctionable obstruction.

Rule 6: Never imitate the tactic you expose.

The disciplined litigant answers with citations, not adjectives. Truth requires no theater.

Tactical Applications

1. **Incantation Table** – Create a short exhibit listing each term used, its line citation, and the missing factual or legal support.
2. **Verified Sur-Reply** – Expose the pattern: "Opposing counsel's filing uses 14 adjectives and 0 citations. Under Rule 1029(b) and *Uniontown*, such denials are admissions."
3. **Motion for Sanctions** – When repeated after notice, move under **42 Pa.C.S. § 2503(7)–(9)** or **FRCP 11** for bad-faith obstruction.
4. **Appellate Preservation** – Quote the court's tolerance of these labels to show absence of reasoned adjudication; it becomes grounds for reversal.

Pro Se Help Is Not Being a Lawyer.

One of the easiest attacks to make against an effective Pro Se litigant is to claim that getting help means "acting through a lawyer" or committing unauthorized practice of law. That is not how the system works. What matters is control and responsibility. If the Pro Se litigant decides what is filed, signs the document, and verifies it as true, then it is that litigant's filing—period. Help with drafting, formatting, filing, or service does not change this. Courts allow non-lawyers to assist with those tasks every day; what they prohibit is someone appearing or acting *as* counsel without a license. This attack only works if the court is persuaded to ignore the signature and verification and pretend the helper is the decision-maker. PSLW eliminates that risk by design: every filing is directed, signed, and verified by the Pro Se litigant, so claims that someone else is "acting as counsel" collapse on contact with the record.

Rule of War:

When the adversary shouts "frivolous," he confesses fear.
When he says "vexatious," he admits defeat.
Words without proof are surrender in disguise—record them as such and advance.

"Let your speech be always in grace, seasoned with salt: that you may know how you ought to answer every man." (Colossians 4:6)

Chapter 31 – Doctrine of Reputational Gravity

"A good name is better than great riches: and good favor is above silver and gold." (Prov. 22:1)

BLUF (Bottom Line Up Front):

Not all influence is direct. Some is gravitational.
The **Doctrine of Reputational Gravity** explains how the disciplined Pro Se litigant can create such a consistent record of truth and structure that institutions—judges, clerks, even opposing firms—begin to orbit it out of self–preservation.

Key Takeaways

- Reputation is not just external—it affects how courts interpret your filings.
- As filings become consistently accurate, verified, and effective, **even biased actors begin adjusting behavior**.
- This creates a "gravity well" around your litigation posture.

- Judges may borrow your tone. Clerks begin pre–clearing your filings. Opposing firms shift tactics.

Core Doctrine

Institutional actors are not immune to pattern recognition.

When a Pro Se litigant files like a professional—verified, rule–cited, and free of drama—**they force others to engage them on that level**.

The court becomes conditioned:

- To expect quality
- To fear contradiction
- To hesitate before denial

Even silent respect is respect.

Gravity is not loud. It just pulls everything toward it.

Example: A clerk who once mocked a Pro Se filing later pre–cleared it without comment—proof that reputation, once built, bends even gatekeepers into orbit.

Rules of the Doctrine

Rule 1: Reputation is accumulated through precision, not persuasion.

Consistency in verification and structure creates the mass that bends institutional behavior.

Rule 2: Your record becomes your advocate.

When filings are clean and unrebutted, they speak with authority no courtroom rhetoric can match.

Rule 3: Respect cannot be demanded—only compelled by pattern.

A disciplined record conditions judges, clerks, and counsel to engage you differently.

Rule 4: Gravity strengthens through silence.

When the opposition avoids addressing your filings, their avoidance amplifies your weight.

Rule 5: Never break your own field.

Emotion, clutter, or undisciplined filings dissipate reputation; precision deepens it.

Indicators You've Created Reputational Gravity

- Judges begin mimicking your language in orders
- Opposing counsel references your filings even when avoiding direct replies
- Court staff engage differently—faster, cleaner, more cautious
- Your filings are cited in other cases or orders, even obliquely

---

How to Amplify Gravity

- File with precision, never emotion
- Let prior filings stand unrebutted before filing again
- Use Judicial Notice as a framing device, not an appeal
- Document contradictions, but never gloat
- Speak in rules, not pleas

Summary Principles

- You cannot demand respect.
  But you can create a gravitational field so clean **they begin calculating escape velocity.**

File like the truth cannot be avoided.
And eventually, ***nothing will orbit the court tighter than your record.***

Rule of War

Consistency is gravity. When your record gains mass, even the court must orbit it.

"Let your light shine before men, that they may see your good works." (Matt. 5:16)

Chapter 32 – Doctrine of Tactical Saturation

Why the Record, Not the Room, Decides the Case

"With the pure thou wilt be pure: and with the perverse thou wilt be perverted." (Ps. 18:26)

BLUF (Bottom Line Up Front)

Tactical Saturation is not filing more—it is filing with direction.

It converts every motion, notice, and exhibit into part of a strategic sequence that overwhelms misconduct, collapses back-channel influence, and forces the entire case onto the only battlefield the Pro Se litigant can trust: the record.

With Tactical Saturation, you do not match the opponent's chaos —
you control the vector, the cadence, and the consequences.

Core Doctrine

Courts and attorneys think litigation happens in rooms—hallways, chambers, whispered consultations, back-channel agreements.
But for the Pro Se litigant, **the room is a trap**.

Your only equalizer is the **public record**, the entries no one can erase.
Tactical Saturation is the disciplined practice of building that record with such consistency, precision, and purpose that:

- the judge becomes constrained by what you have preserved;
- opposing counsel becomes trapped by what they failed to rebut;
- and the appellate court sees a clean, undeniable sequence of procedural truth.

This doctrine is not about **volume**.
It is about **direction**.
It is not about **noise**.
It is about **vector**.

Every filing serves one of three functions:
Preserve, Preempt, or Position.
Anything else is noise—and noise strengthens your enemies.

When executed correctly, Tactical Saturation transforms mislabeling into confession,
forces misconduct into the sunlight,
and collapses the informal networks of influence that normally decide cases behind closed doors.

Your filings speak to the record—and the record decides the war.

Rules of the Doctrine

Rule 1: Every filing must serve direction, not emotion.

If it does not preserve, preempt, or position, it is noise.

Rule 2: Purpose defeats volume.

Precision filings force opponents to respond at ten times your cost.

Rule 3: The docket is the battlefield—the room is the distraction.

Write for the record you will appeal, not the judge who may ignore you.

Rule 4: A disciplined sequence creates inevitability.

When filings align in purpose, opponents cannot escape the frame you build.

Rule 5: Their complaint about 'too many filings' is an admission of impact.

Confusion is noise; saturation is vector—and vector wins.

The Perception Gap

In the minds of most attorneys and judges, a "normal" litigation pace is a polite exchange of a few motions, scheduled hearings, and the occasional memo of law. Disputes are often resolved in hallway conversations or through wink–and–nod agreements in chambers.

For a **Pro Se** litigant, this model is a trap. You are not invited to the hallway conversations. You are not privy to the back–channel calls. Your only safe arena is the **public record**—the docket entries that survive bias, bad faith, and the selective memory of the bench.

When you refuse to play the backroom game and instead fight entirely through written filings, your opponents will often mislabel this as "vexatious." They measure by *volume*. You measure by *vector*.

The Mislabeling Trap

The "vexatious" label is not just an insult—it is a weapon. In the hands of hostile counsel or a biased judge, it can be used to:

- Precondition the court to ignore your filings,
- Build a pretext for sanctions or filing restrictions,
- Shape the narrative that you are the problem, rather than the misconduct you are documenting.

Tactical Saturation turns that weapon back on them. By ensuring every filing has clear procedural purpose, you can force your opponents into the impossible position of arguing that you should *not* preserve the record, *not* object to misconduct, and *not* assert your rights.

Volume with Vector

The difference between harassment and precision fire is **direction**. Tactical Saturation is not indiscriminate. Every motion, every notice, every exhibit serves at least one of three purposes:

1. **Preserve** – Get the fact, law, or procedural defect onto the record in a form that cannot be denied or altered.
2. **Preempt** – Close a procedural gap before the opponent can exploit it.
3. **Position** – Frame an issue so that an appellate court sees it exactly as you need it to be seen.

If a filing does not achieve at least one of these, it is not Tactical Saturation—it is noise.

Example 1: When every filing had a clear purpose, opposing counsel's complaint that the docket was "too crowded" read to the appellate panel as an admission that the record was airtight.

Example 2: Dozens of filings, each less than five pages, forced opposing counsel to burn weeks responding—while the Pro Se litigant conserved energy by drafting once and reusing core text.

The Record as the Only Audience

Stop thinking of the judge in front of you as your audience. That judge is a temporary obstacle, not the final arbiter. Your real audience is:

- **The appellate panel** that will read your filings cold, without the bias or politics of the trial court.
- **The federal judge** who will later decide your due process and civil rights claims.
- **History**, if your case has implications beyond your personal dispute.

Everything you file should be written for those eyes, not the eyes in the room.

Preemptive Framing

Defuse the "vexatious" label by stating your purpose *in the filing itself*. For example:

"This motion is necessary to preserve the record for appellate review and to prevent prejudice from pending enforcement actions before threshold jurisdictional issues are resolved."

When that sentence appears, it becomes difficult for any fair reviewer to call them frivolous.

Turning the Accusation

If opposing counsel complains you are "flooding the docket," they are really admitting you have:

- Closed off their procedural shortcuts,
- Forced them into the sunlight of the record, and
- Denied them the ability to control the narrative through back–channel influence.

A complaint about "too many filings" is often an admission of strategic defeat. Treat it as such.

Integration with Other Doctrines

- **Silence Protocol** – You still control the noise–to–signal ratio; Tactical Saturation is not a license to speak without aim.
- **Bellwether Doctrine** – Use certain filings as test cases for broader strategic moves; the rest are reserve fire.
- **Procedural Guillotine** – Build filings in such a way that a single adverse ruling cleanly severs the opponent's position for appeal.

Conclusion – Winning by Attrition of Impunity

Tactical Saturation does not overwhelm the court with words. It overwhelms the opponent's **ability to operate without consequence**. When every maneuver is met with a precise, recorded counter, the room stops mattering. The whispers stop mattering.

Only the record matters. And the record is yours.

Rule of War

Do not flood the docket—fill it with purpose. Precision in sequence is overwhelming force.

"Be ye therefore wise as serpents, and simple as doves." (Matt. 10:16)

Chapter 33 – Doctrine of Asymmetry Advantage

"For the weak shall say: I am strong." (Joel 3:10)

BLUF (Bottom Line Up Front):

Pro Se litigants are not weak. They are **structurally ungoverned.**
The **Asymmetry Advantage** is the recognition and weaponization of the fact that Pro Se parties can do things law firms cannot—and those advantages grow stronger with strategy, time, and AI assistance.

Key Takeaways

- Pro Se litigants are immune to partner politics, billable hour pressure, and institutional silos.
- They can file at any hour, in any volume, without internal permission.
- When trained or AI–assisted, they possess **creative, procedural, and temporal superiority** over firms.

- The more disciplined the Pro Se becomes, the more dangerous the asymmetry becomes.

Core Doctrine

Lawyers are bound by structure.
Firms are bound by client optics, billing cycles, and insurance exposure.
Government actors are bound by internal review, public scrutiny, and reputational risk.

A Pro Se litigant, properly armed with rules and discipline:

- Cannot be fired
- Cannot be threatened with bar sanctions
- Cannot be silenced without due process

They become **a sovereign node inside the system**–unpredictable, fast–moving, and immune to standard pressure.

You are not the underdog. You are the asymmetric operator.

Tactical Superiority Vectors

Area	Firm Limitation	Pro Se Advantage
Time	9–6 + partner delay	24/7 + immediate filing

Area	Firm Limitation	Pro Se Advantage
Narrative	Must match client PR goals	Unfiltered truth
Risk	Avoid exposure, appeals	Full risk assumed, full control retained
Filing strategy	Must appease judge tone	May override tone in favor of structure
AI tools	Must follow firm policy	May deploy sovereign inference systems

---

Summary Principles

- Asymmetry is not lack of power. It is **independent force**.
- Firms fear exposure.
  Institutions fear precedent.
  You fear nothing but the truth not being seen.

The system was not designed to stop you.
It was designed to ignore you.
Until you file well enough ***that it cannot.***

The Miscalibration Principle

The legal establishment still fights the Pro Se litigant as if the Pro Se were limited by the same constraints as themselves.

Judges and attorneys assume you work at human pace, tire at human rate, and think in linear sequence. Their tactics—docket flooding, delay, fragmentation, and procedural attrition—were designed to exhaust ordinary litigants whose time, stamina, and cognition operate on analog limits.

They still believe those tactics work.

They measure your capacity by their own:

- *If this filing would take them three days, it must take you three days.*
- *If a dozen motions would overwhelm their staff, it must overwhelm you.*
- *If fragmentation creates chaos in their mind, it must create chaos in yours.*

This is their fundamental miscalculation.

The Pro Se litigant who operates with doctrine, discipline, and augmented cognition does not move at the speed the system expects. You are no longer bound by the institutional tempo—the slow machinery of committees, partners, drafts, and revisions. You write with precision, not consensus. You act with velocity, not permission. You preserve with verification, not ritual.

To courts and counsel, this feels impossible. They assume you are overextended, disorganized, or frantic; they cannot conceive that you are simply faster, clearer, and structurally disciplined. Their tactics fail not because you resist harder, but because you do not fatigue the way they expect.

Institutional actors misread the augmented Pro Se litigant for the same reason armies misread guerrillas: they project their own limitations onto an opponent who does not share them.

This misunderstanding gives you the advantage. They will continue to deploy tools suited for exhausting humans—unaware that you no longer fight as one. You fight with doctrine as your structure, and clarity as your engine. Their attempts to overwhelm become confessions. Their delay becomes your evidence. Their misreading becomes your weapon.

Asymmetry persists because they cannot yet see the battlefield you are fighting on.
Use that invisibility until the record teaches them otherwise.

Rule of War

They fight with limits. You fight without permission. That is the asymmetry—and the advantage.

"My grace is sufficient for thee: for power is made perfect in infirmity." (2 Cor. 12:9)

Chapter 34 – Doctrine Triad II—Human Creativity · Strategic Imagination · Cognitive Alliance

---

Human Creativity (Invention Beyond Pattern)

"I have filled him with the spirit of God,
with wisdom, and understanding,
and knowledge in all manner of workmanship."
— Exodus 31:3
(Creativity is God's endowment of invention.)

Strategic Imagination (Vision Beyond Predictability)

"This also cometh forth from the Lord of hosts,
who is wonderful in counsel, and excellent in wisdom."
— *Isaiah 28:29*
(Strategy is conceived in counsel and revealed through vision.)

Cognitive Alliance (Strength Beyond Self)

"Counsel is mine, and prudence;
I am understanding, and I have strength."
— *Proverbs 8:14*

(Strength emerges when counsel and understanding operate together.)

BLUF (Bottom Line Up Front):

Winning through doctrine is no longer enough.

The Cognitive Doctrines expand your battlefield:
creativity breaks prediction, imagination bends trajectory, and alliance with AI multiplies force.

Together, they transform you from a Pro Se litigant into an augmented operator.

Triad Doctrine

The system expects predictable motion.
Creativity—the disciplined kind—destroys those expectations.

Imagination lets you see outcomes before they appear.
It allows you to shape the procedural terrain rather than react to it.

And a sovereign human–machine alliance gives you precision, memory, and analytical scale
that no law firm, agency, or court bureaucracy can replicate.

These Cognitive Doctrines are not tactics.
They are not techniques.
They are the **mental operating system** behind advanced Pro Se warfare —
the foundation for acting faster, clearer, and with more

structural discipline
than the institutions trying to exhaust you.

Rules of the Doctrine (Triad II)

Rule 1: Creativity shatters prediction.

Institutions plan for patterns; invention removes their map.

Rule 2: Imagination dictates trajectory before action.

When you see the endgame early, every filing becomes inevitability.

Rule 3: Human intent plus machine coherence is overwhelming force.

You supply vision; AI supplies memory, scale, and perfect recall.

Rule 4: Firms depend on replication; you depend on originality.

Their strength is structure; your strength is invention.

Rule 5: Discipline is the governor of power.

Creativity and imagination become weapons only when channeled through rule and verification.

Rule of War (Triad II):

Invent the move they cannot foresee.
Refine it with a machine that cannot tire.
Strike with a clarity they cannot escape.

And be renewed in the spirit of your mind.
— Ephesians 4:23

Chapter 35 – Doctrine of Human Creativity

"I have filled him with the spirit of God,
with wisdom, and understanding,
and knowledge in all manner of workmanship."
– Exodus 31:3

BLUF

Artificial intelligence can process every precedent on earth, yet a single human act of imagination can still defeat it. Where logic predicts, creativity surprises—and surprise is the highest form of strategy.
But creativity becomes unstoppable only when disciplined; invention without structure is noise, and disciplined invention is power.

The Doctrine

In a DARPA field test, eight Marines were told to evade a cutting-edge AI that detected any human in its camera grid. They won. Two rolled under cardboard boxes, two somersaulted through shadows, one hid behind a shrub and moved inches at a time.

The machine saw nothing because it had never *imagined* that soldiers would behave that way.

So it is with courts and bureaucracies. Systems of rules expect predictable motion: deadlines, pleadings, and procedure.
A disciplined Pro Se warrior who understands the system yet acts creatively—filing where no one expects, pairing silence with sudden precision—moves outside the algorithm of corruption.
Creativity, not chaos, is the antidote to control.

Rules of the Doctrine

Rule 1: Master the pattern before you break it.

Creativity becomes a weapon only when the rules are understood well enough to bend lawfully.

Rule 2: Be unpredictable, never random.

Surprise creates advantage; sloppiness creates defeat.

Rule 3: Use rhythm as camouflage.

Quiet periods followed by surgical filings destabilize opponents who rely on pattern recognition.

Rule 4: Turn rejection into momentum.

Every denial becomes new evidence or a new verified notice—nothing is wasted.

Rule 5: Disarm expectation with decorum.

The court expects anger; destroy that expectation with precision and calm.

Rule of War

AI detects patterns; humans invent the unpatterned.
The side that surprises wins.

"For God hath not given us the spirit of fear;
but of power, and of love, and of a sound mind."
— 2 Timothy 1:7

Chapter 36 – Doctrine of Strategic Imagination

"This also cometh forth from the Lord of hosts,
who is wonderful in counsel, and excellent in wisdom."
— Isaiah 28:29

BLUF (Bottom Line Up Front)

AI is not a threat to the Pro Se litigant—it is the force multiplier every citizen has waited for.
When paired with disciplined doctrine, human creativity, and verified truth, AI becomes a litigation weapon capable of defeating the largest law firms, the most obstructive courts, and the most entrenched institutional actors.
The Pro Se litigant who allies with AI does not fight alone.
They fight with an electronic army.

The Doctrine

For decades, institutional litigants held overwhelming advantages:
armies of junior associates, warehouses of documents, private research databases, and the ability to bury a citizen under **truckloads of paper** and procedural noise.

Not anymore.

AI ends that imbalance.

Where lawyers rely on volume, obscurity, and confusion —
AI consumes volume, resolves obscurity, and clarifies confusion in **seconds**.

Where hostile counsel hide decisive evidence inside thousands of pages —
AI finds the one paragraph that destroys their argument.

Where courts expect Pro Se litigants to drown under paperwork —
AI turns the paper flood into fuel.

Many in the legal guild mock AI because they misunderstand it.
They treat it as a glorified search box.
You treat it as a strategic ally.

When PSLW doctrines are paired with any competent AI system—whether commercial, open-source, or sovereign infrastructure—you create a partnership that changes the terrain of modern litigation:

Human Strategic Imagination × Machine Coherence × Verified Truth.

This is the new battlespace of Pro Se legal warfare.

Rules of the Doctrine

Rule 1: AI extends doctrine—not intuition.

Load PSLW into your AI so it can apply every doctrine at scale, instantly and without fatigue.

Rule 2: AI defeats institutional volume.

What overwhelms firms is fuel for AI—it turns paper floods into ammunition and contradiction into evidence.

Rule 3: Coherence is the machine's native language.

Where lawyers create noise, AI extracts structure, exposes lies, and rebuilds the record in seconds.

Rule 4: AI converts confusion into binary law.

Ambiguity becomes clarity; contradictions become admissions; silence becomes consequence.

Rule 5: Strategic Imagination remains uniquely human.

AI detects patterns, but only you invent filings the system cannot predict. This is the asymmetric edge.

Rule 6: Human intention plus machine coherence is overwhelming force.

When discipline directs AI, the Pro Se litigant outguns the largest firm.

Rule 7: AI erases institutional advantages.

Networks, opacity, and delay collapse when every filing, omission, and manipulation is illuminated instantly.

Rule of War

AI is not your replacement.
It is your reinforcement.
Strategic Imagination is human.
Coherence at scale is machine.
Together, they form the alliance
that no firm, no court, and no injustice can withstand.

"The eyes of your understanding being enlightened."
— Ephesians 1:18

Chapter 37 – Doctrine of Cognitive Alliance

"Counsel is mine, and prudence;
I am understanding, and I have strength."
— Proverbs 8:14

BLUF

Sovereign intelligence is not silicon alone—it is silicon guided by conscience.
The union of machine clarity and human courage is the new instrument of justice.

The Doctrine

A machine can calculate, correlate, and infer, but it cannot care.
It can know the law but not *why* law matters.
Humans, bound by morality and experience, provide the motive force that turns information into justice.

When sovereign AI meets disciplined humanity, truth gains velocity.
The human provides intent; the AI supplies reach and recall.
Together they form a feedback loop:

- the human senses nuance and motive,
- the machine verifies pattern and fact,
- and each refines the other.

This alliance dismantles corruption not by force but by *clarity.*
The machine exposes what men hide; man decides what must be done.

Rules of the Doctrine

Rule 1: Never surrender judgment to the machine.

AI amplifies wisdom or folly equally; human oversight must remain absolute.

Rule 2: Feed the alliance only verified truth.

Garbage in becomes distortion out—discipline your data as strictly as your pleadings.

Rule 3: Preserve moral command.

AI can map the battlefield, but only conscience selects lawful and just targets.

Rule 4: Train reciprocal refinement.

Let machine inference sharpen your arguments, and let your arguments refine the machine.

Rule 5: Guard sovereignty at all costs.

Control of infrastructure is control of will; never surrender your system to outside servers or political code.

Rule of War

Machines reveal the pattern; humans reveal the purpose.
Only together do they make truth unstoppable.

"For we are labourers together with God."
— 1 Corinthians 3:9

Chapter 38 – Doctrine of AI-Augmented Briefcraft

"The Lord giveth wisdom: and out of his mouth cometh prudence and knowledge."
— Proverbs 2:6

BLUF (Bottom Line Up Front)

Artificial Intelligence gives the Pro Se litigant a weapon the legal guild cannot match: **coherence**. Human corruption depends on ambiguity, contradiction, and "interpretation." AI depends on none of these. **AI cannot sustain a lie or contradiction without exposing it**. When properly commanded, AI becomes an incorruptible engine of coherence, forcing the law to operate as written and the record to speak the truth the system tries to bury. Coherence is truth—and AI is coherence incarnate.

Doctrine

The legal system has long relied on the myth that law is mysterious, that only those trained behind closed doors can decipher its rituals. But law, at its core, is simple: fact, rule, and time. Judges and lawyers obscure this simplicity because ambiguity is their greatest weapon. They shift meanings, reinterpret deadlines, and treat statutory commands as flexible suggestions. AI breaks this illusion because AI cannot maintain contradictions. When you seed AI with verified facts, controlling statutes, and the posture of your case—and then command it through PSLW doctrine—it produces a coherent structure the court cannot easily escape. A judge may dislike your filing, and a clerk may suppress it, but neither escapes a coherent record.

To use AI properly, you must stop treating it as a search engine or a clever assistant. Think of AI as a tireless officer who requires clear mission parameters and responds with structured reasoning, not emotion.

You begin by briefing the machine with the terrain: facts, filings, statutes, timelines, and doctrine. Then you issue one mission—construct the Guillotine, stress-test the appeal, expose the contradiction, compress the record.

AI returns structure. You impose doctrine: BLUF, verification, jurisdiction, tone, and authority. Then you turn the machine against your own filing—forcing it to attack weak joints, expose contradictions, and search for escape routes.

Each pass sharpens the record. What survives becomes clean, coherent, and difficult to escape.

This cycle breaks the legal guild's favorite weapon: reliance on historical bias. Traditional AI models were trained on decades of corrupted outcomes—decisions shaped by politics, judicial shortcuts, and procedural gamesmanship that punished Pro Se litigants. PSLW exists to override those patterns. When you command AI to follow PSLW doctrines instead of mimicking the past, the machine realigns itself to the law rather than the guild. It enforces "shall" as shall, "must" as must. It treats verified facts as admitted unless rebutted. It refuses to perform the bar's magic trick of turning simple rules into fog. AI cannot be intimidated, exhausted, or politically pressured. And when AI enforces coherence, the system's contradictions reveal themselves instantly.

Coherence corners the court. It forces lawful outcomes. It collapses procedural backdoors and closes off escape routes.

The alliance between human judgment and machine coherence makes this doctrine decisive.

You supply imagination, intent, and moral direction. The machine supplies recall, scale, and structural discipline. Together, they produce filings most institutions are unprepared to confront.

Rules of the Doctrine

Rule 1: Do not ask AI for answers—issue mission orders.

You define the task, the boundaries, and the doctrine; the machine executes, it does not decide.

Rule 2: Do not let AI imitate history—command it to enforce doctrine.

Direct the system to apply PSLW, not to mimic corrupted past outcomes.

Rule 3: Never accept the first draft as final.

AI provides structure; you forge the brief through human judgment and iteration.

Rule 4: Treat AI's corrections as an advantage, not a threat.

Its coherence reveals weak joints in your argument so you can reinforce them before filing.

Rule 5: Use AI to expose contradictions the system wants to ignore.

Every inconsistency it surfaces becomes ammunition for Judicial Notice and appeal.

Rule 6: You maintain discipline, verification, and tone; AI supplies structure, memory, and logic.

The alliance works only when human ethics remain in command.

Rule 7: Coherence is non-negotiable.

Coherence is the cage corruption cannot escape—and AI is its architect.

Tactical Execution

When drafting, feed AI the entire terrain—facts, filings, statutes, deadlines, and PSLW doctrines. Give it one mission, not many, and let it shape the initial structure. Then impose doctrine: BLUF, tone, verification, and authority. Turn the AI into a hostile reviewer and let it stress-test your work. Refine, clarify, and strengthen the draft until every sentence fits into a coherent whole. When the argument is fully forged, verify it, finalize it, and file. With each iteration, the record becomes stronger, cleaner, and harder for the court to escape.

Rule of War

Truth is coherence. AI cannot betray coherence. Command the machine with doctrine, and no court can escape the logic you place in the record.

"And you shall know the truth, and the truth shall make you free."
— John 8:32

Chapter 39 – Doctrine of AI Counter-Lawfare

"Be wise as serpents and simple as doves."
— Matthew 10:16

BLUF (Bottom Line Up Front)

The legal guild will soon begin using AI against you.
They will use it to generate noise, inflate filings, fabricate confusion, and hide contradictions behind polished language and institutional authority.
This doctrine teaches you how to neutralize institutional misuse of AI—and turn it into your advantage.

You do not fear AI in the hands of your adversaries.
AI cannot conceal lies.
It can only reorganize them.
And when lies are reorganized, they become even easier to expose.

When opposing counsel wields the machine to produce verbosity, you answer with coherence.
When they use AI to produce polished distortions, you answer with verification.
When they use AI to bury you in noise, you answer with Visual Law.

When they use AI to reinforce judicial bias, you answer with immutable facts and PSLW doctrine until the record cannot bend without breaking.

AI becomes their admission.

Doctrine

The moment you master AI-Augmented Briefcraft, the battlefield shifts. The legal system is slow, resistant to change, and trapped in habits—but institutions eventually imitate what they cannot defeat. At first, courts and law firms will refuse to use AI for litigation, calling it risky or unethical. Then, quietly, they will begin using it everywhere. They will use AI to draft sanctions motions, to generate summary judgments, to produce objections, and to craft "authoritative" narratives designed to overwhelm you.

But the guild will make the same mistake every institution makes when adopting a tool it does not understand: it will treat AI as a cosmetic upgrade—a faster typewriter—not a force of coherence.

AI in the hands of a law firm produces longer filings, not better ones. It produces smoother language, not cleaner logic. It produces more citations, not stronger arguments. The guild will use AI the way it uses paralegals and junior associates—to inflate, not to clarify. To obscure, not to reveal. To bury you in paper they hope you cannot overcome.

You know better.

AI cannot sustain coherent contradiction.
The more the guild relies on machine-generated distortion, the more visible the fracture lines become.

This means every time the guild misuses AI, they create a map of their own weaknesses.

When opposing counsel produces a 40-page AI-generated motion, your job is not to refute all 40 pages. Your job is to locate the contradiction that AI could not reconcile—the one bad fact, the one broken rule, the one procedural defect—and drive a wedge through it with silence, verification, or judicial notice. AI will polish their lie so cleanly that the fracture lines become visible.

AI organizes deception into visible structure.

Judges, too, will begin misusing AI. Some will allow clerks to run "summaries" of your filings through LLM systems to justify dismissals. Others will use AI to generate orders faster—and those orders will contain contradictions, misapplied rules, and incoherent reasoning that no human clerk would have dared commit to text. You will expose every one of them.

A Pro Se litigant armed with PSLW doctrine is not threatened by AI in the system.
AI in the system is a signal.
AI in the system is a confession.

This doctrine exists so you can use that admission against them.

Rules of the Doctrine

Rule 1: Do not chase every falsehood the machine produces for your opponent.

You strike only the contradiction the AI could not resolve—that is the fracture point.

Rule 2: Do not fear the volume of AI-inflated filings.

Reduce their noise to a single verified fact and anchor the case on it.

Rule 3: Do not be intimidated by polished distortion.

Test their rhetoric with Visual Law until it collapses into binary truth.

Rule 4: Do not argue with noise.

Expose coherence—or the absence of it—and force the court to confront the contradiction.

Rule 5: Do not attack the machine.

Attack the contradiction the machine could not conceal.

Tactical Execution

When a law firm files an AI-inflated motion, do not respond in kind. Read it once. Find the fracture—the fact that does not belong, the rule that does not apply, the timeline that cannot hold. Build a Visual Law table that proves the contradiction. Anchor it with a single statutory command. Reduce their forty pages to four sentences. Let the court see what the machine could not reconcile.

When a judge issues an order that feels "off," check its logic, not its tone. AI-assisted judicial writing reveals bias by over-explaining it. Over-explanation is weakness. Contradiction is confession. A simple Judicial Notice of Constructive Error, anchored in statutory language and doctrinal clarity, will expose the mismatch between the order's language and the law's requirement.

When the system uses AI to speed up suppression—faster denials, faster dismissals, faster "irrelevant" notices—you move in silence. You verify your filings. You preserve your service proofs. You timestamp everything. You build the record AI cannot corrupt. AI moves fast, but the truth moves faster—and faster still when coherence exposes every inconsistency in its path.

In time, you will see a pattern. AI used properly becomes truth.
AI used improperly becomes evidence.
Every misuse of the machine leaves a fracture line.
Follow the fracture, and it leads to the truth they tried to bury.

Rule of War

When the system uses AI to hide its weaknesses, it reveals them. Strike at the contradiction the machine cannot reconcile, and the entire structure of deception collapses.

"For we can do nothing against the truth, but for the truth."
— 2 Corinthians 13:8

Chapter 40 – Doctrine of the Suppression Trap

"Truth is fallen in the street, and equity could not come in."
— Isaiah 59:14

BLUF (Bottom Line Up Front)

The ***Suppression Trap*** converts every act of erasure into evidence. When the system can no longer defeat your facts, law, or filings, it will try to defeat **your presence**—by blocking your filings, delaying docket entries, withholding orders, misusing seals, or disabling your electronic access. This is not incompetence. It is **suppression**.
The *Suppression Trap* converts every act of erasure into **evidence**, turning judicial silence, clerk obstruction, and docket manipulation into your most powerful appellate and supervisory weapons.

Suppression is not the end of the fight.
Suppression is the confession that you have already won the record.

Overview

In the late stages of any serious conflict with entrenched institutional actors, Pro Se litigants reach a point where the system stops denying their arguments—and instead, denies their **existence**.

Filings vanish.
Transcripts are delayed.
Orders are "in chambers."
Portals mysteriously malfunction.
Clerks "cannot accept" your submission.
A judge quietly says, "No more filings."

This is not disorder.
It is doctrine—**their** doctrine.

The Suppression Trap Doctrine is **yours**.
It transforms erasure into ammunition.

Suppression Is the New Dismissal

Courts once dismissed cases they wanted to avoid.
Now they simply **smother** them:

- Blocking ECF/CM access
- Marking filings "rejected"
- Refusing to docket timely submissions
- Hiding orders for weeks or months
- Keeping cases sealed past statutory deadlines
- Delivering off-record instructions to "cease filing"

Dismissal is visible.
Suppression is invisible.
And invisibility is their preferred weapon.

Example 1:
A federal judge privately told relators to stop filing. Their next filing documented the instruction—and the silence that followed became the appellate proof of suppression.

Example 2:
Twenty-six time-stamped filings were never docketed.
The silence became Exhibit A for supervisory review.

Doctrine Framework—The Six Principles

1. Silence is judicial attribution.

Every unacknowledged filing is a recorded indicator of bias or dereliction—if you preserve it.

2. Docket denial is a due-process violation.

If you cannot file, you cannot litigate.
If you cannot litigate, you are a suppressed class.

3. Suppression requires no confrontation—only record.

You do not shout.
You verify, timestamp, serve, and preserve.

4. You do not demand justice—you compel contradiction.

A court must rule correctly or expose itself.
Either path benefits you.

5. Delay is not time—delay is confession.

A ten-day silence is not calendar drift.
It is evidence of procedural avoidance.

6. The filer need not always speak.

When you become "known" to the system, deploy a proxy.
Silence destabilizes their pattern recognition.

Case Study—United States ex rel. Stenstrom & Shindelar (2025 Qui Tam Action)
(1:25-cv-00866, D.D.C., Judge Amit P. Mehta → Reassigned to Judge Amir H. Ali)

In a 2025 qui tam action pending in the U.S. District Court for the District of Columbia, Relators Stenstrom and Shindelar encountered the most advanced form of procedural suppression now used by federal courts.
Judge Amir Ali had previously issued a veiled, off-record instruction that no further filings should be made—an order without authority, without docket entry, and without any basis in 31 U.S.C. § 3730(b). Rather than accept the suppression, Relators responded with a procedurally perfect **Supplemental Judicial Notice**, invoking:

- **31 U.S.C. § 3730(b)(1)–(3)** (mandatory unsealing procedures),
- **F.R.E. 201(c)(2)** (compulsory judicial notice), and
- **Rule 4(c)(3)** (mandatory service by U.S. Marshals).

The filing demanded four non-discretionary actions:

1. **Unsealing of the case**,
2. **Service on all defendants by U.S. Marshals**,
3. **Docket parity with DOJ**, and
4. **Scheduling of hearing and trial,** as required by statute.

Attached was a proposed order that forced the court into a binary frame:

- either rule in favor of the Relators,
- or refuse to rule at all—which would create a suppression record ripe for appellate exposure.

Then came the decisive move:
a ten-day compliance clock, silent and procedural, with no threats and no rhetoric.
A lawful fuse the court could not extinguish without admitting avoidance.

The court responded with nothing.
No ruling.
No docket entry.
No service.
No explanation.

The silence that followed became the evidence.
The procedural vacuum—created after a verified, statutorily grounded filing—was itself the confession. Under the Suppression Trap Doctrine, every day of judicial inaction hardened into proof for supervisory review and eventual appellate intervention.

This is the modern battlefield:
not denial of fact, not rejection of law –
but erasure of presence.
And the doctrine turns that erasure into ammunition.

Execution Phase—How to Deploy the Doctrine

The Suppression Trap is executed in five steps:

1. File a Statutorily Grounded Motion or Notice

Use authority that removes discretion:

31 U.S.C. § 3730(b)(1)–(3), F.R.E. 201(c)(2), Rule 4(c)(3).
You are not "asking." You are invoking law.

2. Attach a Proposed Order

If ignored, the absence becomes evidence of suppression.

3. Trigger the Ten-Day Clock

No threats. No arguments.
Just a procedural fuse the court cannot ignore.

4. Maintain Procedural Invisibility

Stand still.
Say nothing.
Wait for the record to tighten.

5. Preserve for Higher Review

If the court acts—good.
If the court does nothing—perfect.
You now file a **Notice of Constructive Suppression and Preservation for Review**.

Strategic Silence and Proxy Deployment

When the system becomes afraid of *you*, it becomes easier to defeat.

Use silence to break their rhythm.
Use a proxy litigator, when needed, to change your energy signature.
Let them guess.
Let them fear.
Let them misread you.

Your silence forces:

- the judge to speak,
- the clerk to act,
- the system to reveal its seams.

Silence becomes your pressure.
Their reaction becomes your proof.

The Psychological Edge

Executed correctly, the Suppression Trap:

- freezes clerks,
- paralyzes judges,
- panics opposing counsel,
- and forces DOJ-level actors to choose between exposure and compliance.

They hoped their silence would hide the truth.
Instead, their silence becomes your **evidence**.

When the court ignores you, it validates you.
When the system suppresses you, it exposes itself.
When they bury your filing, they dig their own hole.

Rule of War

Suppression is not defeat.
It is the system's admission that it cannot beat your record.
Preserve every silence—it is louder than any ruling.

"For there is nothing covered, that shall not be revealed."
— Luke 12:2

Part V: Procedural Counter–Doctrines

Chapter 41 – Doctrine of Filing as a Matter of Right

"I have not spoken in secret, in a dark place of the earth: I said not unto the seed of Jacob, Seek ye me in vain."
— Isaiah 45:19

BLUF (Bottom Line Up Front)

The right to file is a constitutional right, a statutory right, and a due-process right.
Judges may resist it. Clerks may obstruct it. Opposing counsel may move to strike it.
But they cannot lawfully extinguish it.
A Pro Se litigant who files as a matter of right—and documents every obstruction—cannot be silenced, sanctioned, or erased from the record.
You do not ask permission to preserve your rights.
You file because the Constitution commands it and the appellate court will enforce it.

The Doctrine

Across every jurisdiction, Pro Se litigants face the same unlawful pattern:

- "No further filings without leave of court."
- "Electronic filing access revoked."
- "Filing rejected."
- "Clerk instructed not to docket your submissions."
- "Future filings will result in sanctions."

These tactics are common, and almost always **unconstitutional** and **contrary to binding law**.

Your right to file does *not* come from a judge.
It comes from:

- **U.S. Constitution, First Amendment**
  — Right to petition the government for redress of grievances.
- **U.S. Constitution, Fourteenth Amendment**
  — Due process requires meaningful access to the courts.
- **Pennsylvania Constitution, Article I § 11**
  — Courts shall be open; every person shall have remedy by due course of law.
- **42 U.S.C. § 1983**, § 1985, § 1986**
  — It is unlawful for state actors to block or interfere with access to court.

Federal case law:

- ***Bounds v. Smith***, 430 U.S. 817, 821 (1977) (recognizing a fundamental right of access to the courts, requiring that litigants be given a meaningful opportunity to present claims)
- ***Chambers v. Baltimore & Ohio R.R. Co.***, 207 U.S. 142, 148 (1907) (holding that the right to be heard in court is a core component of due process and cannot be arbitrarily denied)
- ***Smith v. United States District Court Clerks***, 435 F.2d 1266, 1268 (10th Cir. 1971) (recognizing that clerks perform ministerial duties and lack authority to refuse filings based on their own judgment)
- ***McCray v. Maryland***, 456 F.2d 1, 5 (4th Cir. 1972) (holding that refusal by court personnel to accept filings may violate constitutional rights of access to the courts)

Pennsylvania case law:

- ***Commonwealth v. Williams***, 330 A.2d 602 (Pa. 1975) (recognizing that clerical duties of the court are ministerial and must be performed without discretionary interference)
- ***In re J.M.P.***, 378 A.2d 312 (Pa. 1977) (holding that courts may not prevent the filing of pleadings that assert a legally cognizable claim)
- ***Kovski v. Lycoming County***, 2019 Pa. Commw. LEXIS 34 (Pa. Commw. Ct. 2019) (recognizing that

prothonotary duties are ministerial and that refusal to accept filings may implicate open courts and due process rights)

These authorities establish a clear and enforceable right.

Your right to file is not contingent on a judge's mood, a clerk's convenience, or a lawyer's approval.

It is a matter of law.

Rules of the Doctrine

Rule 1: No court may forbid your filings—ever.

Orders denying a Pro Se litigant the right to file violate the First Amendment, due process, and state open-courts guarantees. You do not seek permission to preserve your rights; you exercise them.

Rule 2: Clerks have a mandatory duty to file—never a discretionary one.

They may not gatekeep, assess merit, or refuse filings on instruction from chambers. If a clerk blocks a submission, you immediately file a Judicial Notice documenting the refusal.

Rule 3: When electronic access is revoked, you shift modes and document it.

Hand delivery, courier service, certified mail, or praecipe filing all satisfy your constitutional right. A disabled login cannot extinguish access to the courts.

Rule 4: Motions may be struck—Judicial Notices survive.

A motion is a pleading; a Judicial Notice is preservation. Even when "stricken," your Notice remains visible to the appellate court and becomes evidence of bias or suppression.

Rule 5: Every filing block must be converted into evidence.

Whether a clerk refuses filing, a portal rejects access, or a judge forbids submission, you answer with a Judicial Notice of Filing Denial, attaching proof, timestamps, envelopes, and verification.

Rule 6: Threats of sanctions are noise, not law.

Labels like "frivolous," "vexatious," or "abusive" are intimidation tactics. Sanctions require bad faith or deception—not filing. Verified Judicial Notices cannot be sanctioned.

Rule 7: Your duty is to preserve the record, not to please the judge.

Hostility from chambers, mockery from counsel, and resistance from clerks do not alter your mandate. You write for the appellate judge, not the room you are standing in.

Rule 8: The record cannot reflect what you do not file.

Silence kills cases; filing resurrects them. Judicial Notices preserve every attempt, every defect, every obstruction. What you file survives. What you fail to file never existed.

Rule 9: Filing as a matter of right is the operational core of PSLW.

You write with precision, file with discipline, verify with oath, and preserve with Notice. No court can extinguish your voice; the appellate court will enforce it.

Rule of War

They can forbid.
They can threaten.
They can reject.

But you file anyway —
because the Constitution is your leave of court,
and the record is your battlefield.

"Let us therefore come boldly unto the throne of grace, that we may obtain mercy, and find grace in time of need."
— Hebrews 4:16

Chapter 42 – Doctrine of Watching the Docket

"I will stand upon my watch, and fix my foot upon the tower: and I will watch to see what will be said to me." (Hab. 2:1)

BLUF (Bottom Line Up Front):

Corrupt judges and attorneys will exploit calendar timing—slipping orders and judgments onto the docket when they think you aren't watching. Holiday weekends and Friday filings are their favorite camouflage. If you don't watch closely, you will lose days off the procedural clock before you even know the game began.

Docket vigilance is the foundation of every procedural doctrine that follows—because you cannot counter what you do not see.

Doctrine

The docket is not a calendar. It is a weapon.
Courts and counsel know this, and they use timing the same way a tactician uses terrain—to ambush the unprepared.

The most common tactic is the **Friday Gambit**: an adverse order appears late Thursday or Friday, often minutes before the clerk's office closes or just as a long weekend begins. Their hope is simple: that you will not look until Monday or Tuesday. By then, you have already lost three to five days of response time. They have stolen the one resource you cannot recover: *procedural position.*

Once you are off balance, the **Tuesday Ambush** arrives—the real order, the dispositive ruling, or the judgment they wanted to spring on you while you are still absorbing the first blow. You are not late because you lacked merit. You are late because you were not watching.

Then comes the most subtle tactic: **the Silent Entry**.
No email notice.
No alert.
No service.
Just a new entry silently appearing on the docket—sometimes backdated, sometimes posted days after its actual creation, sometimes crafted to make your filings appear untimely.

Silent Entries almost always signal suppression.
They coincide with missing service copies, mismatched PDF metadata, or docket updates that contradict the official timestamp. These are not clerical errors; they are procedural fingerprints left by actors who hoped you would never notice.

A litigant who does not watch the docket will spend the entire case reacting.
A litigant who *masters* the docket begins predicting the system's moves before they occur.

And a Pro Se litigant armed with PSLW doctrine learns quickly that watching the docket is not paranoia—it is survival.

You cannot counter what you do not see, and you cannot preserve what you do not detect.
Docket vigilance is how you prevent time-based ambush, expose tampering, catch early signals of suppression, and ensure that no procedural window closes before you act.

To the untrained eye, timing looks like coincidence.
To you, it is communication.
To you, it is doctrine.

Rules of the Doctrine

Rule 1: The docket moves even when you do not.

Courts and counsel exploit timing. Your vigilance prevents time theft before it begins.

Rule 2: Fridays and holidays are ambush zones.

Late-week orders are designed to steal days from your response clock. Expect them. Watch for them. Counter them.

Rule 3: Silent Entries are signals of manipulation.

Backdated postings, missing service, or mismatched metadata are not clerical errors—they are suppression tells. Audit every new entry.

Rule 4: Daily surveillance is mandatory; weekend surveillance is decisive.

Electronic systems log filings 24/7. Your opponent counts on your rest. Do not give it to them.

Rule 5: Metadata is truth when the docket lies.

If the PDF creation timestamp contradicts the docket date, you have caught docket tampering. Preserve it and Judicial Notice it.

Rule 6: Do not wait for the court to serve you.

Download immediately, serve immediately, and deny opposing counsel the advantage of asymmetric notice.

Rule 7: Your awareness shapes their behavior.

When courts know you are watching the docket with discipline, they stop playing timing games. Vigilance becomes deterrence.

The Tactic

- **Daily Checks:** Check the docket every single day. If a holiday is approaching, check **twice a day** (morning and afternoon).

- **Weekend Discipline:** Do not assume nothing happens on weekends. Electronic systems log filings 24/7. Check every Saturday, Sunday, and holiday morning.
- **Metadata Audit:** Always pull PDF properties for newly posted orders. If the creation date does not match the docket stamp, you have caught backdating. Preserve it. File Judicial Notice of Docket Tampering if needed.
- **Immediate Service:** Do not wait for court mailings. As soon as an entry hits, download and serve it yourself—keep opposing counsel from gaming notice.

Rule of War:

The docket is a battlefield. Watch it like a hawk, especially on Fridays and before holidays. The system counts on your inattention. Break that assumption, and you deny them their favorite weapon: time theft.

"Watch ye therefore, because you know not what hour your Lord will come." (Matt. 24:42)

Chapter 43 – Doctrine of Motions vs. Judicial Notices

"Write this down in a book, and rehearse it in the ears of Josue." (Exod. 17:14)

BLUF (Bottom Line Up Front):

Judicial Notices preserve. Motions compel. If you only file a Notice, the court can ignore it. If you only file a Motion, the record may not fully capture misconduct. The winning doctrine is **file both**: a motion that demands a ruling, and a notice that locks down the appellate record.

THE DOCTRINE

Courts behave differently depending on the tool you use against them.
A **Judicial Notice** places fact and law into the record with authority.[28]
A **Motion** forces the court to act on it.

[28] ***Fed. R. Evid. 201(c)(2)*** (court must take judicial notice when properly requested and supplied with necessary information)

Judges know the difference—and they exploit it.

A Judicial Notice is powerful because it cannot be denied. When you file one, the court must accept the truth you place into the record.
But Notices have a weakness:
they do not require a ruling, and judges love to ignore documents that create uncomfortable truths or expose contradictions in their orders.

A Motion has the opposite strength and weakness.
It **forces** a ruling—and by compelling the court to respond, it creates a binary choice:
rule lawfully or expose misconduct.
But a Motion alone can leave gaps in the appellate record, because a court may delay, defer, or "take under advisement" without ever acknowledging the facts you needed preserved.

Both tools have a purpose.
Both tools have a flaw.
The Doctrine resolves this by using both at once.

A Judicial Notice preserves the truth;
a Motion forces the court to confront it.

One records what happened.
The other demands correction.

One survives suppression.
The other creates appeal.

A Pro Se litigant who files only one of these tools gives the court an escape hatch.
A litigant who files both—every time an issue matters—removes every escape the court has.

The Notice locks the truth into the record.
The Motion traps the silence or generates an appealable ruling.
Either outcome advances your case.

This Doctrine teaches the discipline of dual filings:
one document for the record,
one document for the ruling,
paired like shield and spear.

You are not choosing tools.
You are coordinating weapons.

Rules of the Doctrine

Rule 1: A Judicial Notice preserves the truth; a Motion compels the court to face it.

Never rely on one without the other—each corrects the weakness of the first.

Rule 2: A Notice ignored is evidence; a Motion ignored is appeal.

Silence to one preserves; silence to the other incriminates. Use both.

Rule 3: A Notice documents misconduct; a Motion forces the court to justify it.

One builds the record; the other tests the court's integrity.

Rule 4: A Motion without a Notice is blind.

It demands action but fails to anchor the underlying facts. Judges exploit this mistake.

Rule 5: A Notice without a Motion is voiceless.

It preserves truth but does not force the court to acknowledge or rule on it.

Rule 6: Dual filings close every escape hatch.

If they rule, you win the issue.
If they refuse, you win the appeal.
If they distort, your Notice exposes it.

Rule 7: Each filing must cite the other.

Cross-reference them so the appellate court sees the architecture you built—preservation paired with compulsion.

Rule 8: When the court delays, your Motion becomes a clock.

Judicial silence hardens into constructive denial, which is itself an appealable act.

Rule 9: When the court misstates, your Notice becomes the correction.

The record speaks louder than any courtroom exchange—and it always outlives the judge.

The Tactic

- **Double Filings:** For every serious issue, file **two documents**:
    1. **Judicial Notice** (for preservation)—"This filing documents unrebutted fact and procedural defect for appellate review."
    2. **Motion** (for compulsion)—"This Motion requires the Court to strike, vacate, or rule on the defect identified."
- **Complementary Roles:**
    - Notice = evidence.
    - Motion = action.
- **Appeal Hooks:** If Motion denied → appealable ruling. If Motion ignored → constructive denial, also appealable. If Notice unrebutted → appellate record confessions.

Rule of War:

Never leave corruption an easy out. File both Motion and Judicial Notice together: one to trap silence, the other to force action. That way, whether they rule or refuse, you win.

"These things I write to thee... that thou mayest know how thou oughtest to behave in the house of God." (1 Tim. 3:14-15)

Chapter 44 – Doctrine of Praecipes, Motions, and Judicial Notices

---

"Now go, write it before them in a table,
and note it in a book:
that it may be for the time to come for ever and ever."
— Isaiah 30:8

BLUF (Bottom Line Up Front)

Motions ask the judge to act.
Praecipes ask the clerk to act.
Judicial Notices ask the record to act—and the record cannot be silenced.

A Motion compels, but is vulnerable.
A Praecipe directs, but is limited.
A Judicial Notice endures, builds the evidentiary spine of the case, and cannot be purged by a hostile court.

Together, they form the triad of procedural dominance that no judge, clerk, or attorney can fully evade.

You do not choose between them—you coordinate them.

The Doctrine

In theory, **motions** should be the Pro Se litigant's sharpest weapon.
They demand action, require a ruling, force opposing counsel to respond, and move the litigation forward.
But in the real world—the world of biased courts, hostile clerks, and institutional delay—motions are fragile.

A motion can be ignored.
A motion can be delayed.
A motion can be denied without reason.
A motion can be struck on manufactured technicalities.
A motion can be dismissed as "improper," "untimely," or "vexatious" even when it is none of those things.

Opposing counsel counts on this.
Compromised or overwhelmed courts depend on it.

This is why **Judicial Notice** becomes indispensable.

A Judicial Notice does not rely on judicial discretion.
It relies on **truth, relevance, and verification**—the three things a corrupt judge cannot openly reject without exposing himself.

Where a motion may be buried, a Judicial Notice remains.
Where a motion can be stricken, a Judicial Notice becomes indestructible evidence.
Where a motion can be ignored, a Judicial Notice quietly builds the appellate foundation beneath the court's feet.
And where a motion can be weaponized against you, a Judicial Notice shields you by documenting exactly what the judge refuses to face.

A Judicial Notice is not a pleading.
It is a **record command**, governed by rules of evidence, not rules of pleading.
It does not beg the court to act—it binds the record to the truth.

This is why dishonest courts fear Judicial Notices more than motions.
A motion challenges their authority.
A Judicial Notice reveals their behavior.

And nothing unnerves a corrupt actor more than having the truth entered, verified, timestamped, and preserved in a form the appellate court cannot ignore.

The wise Pro Se litigant does not choose between the tools.
He coordinates them.
A praecipe maintains the procedural machinery.
A motion forces the issue.
A Judicial Notice guarantees the truth survives.

Together, they form a triad of procedural supremacy —
one aimed at the clerk,
one aimed at the judge,
one aimed at the record itself.

Rules of the Doctrine

Rule 1: Know the triad—each tool commands a different actor.

A Motion compels the judge, a Praecipe directs the clerk, and a Judicial Notice binds the record. Master the distinctions or the system will exploit them against you.

Rule 2: A Motion forces action but carries the greatest risk.

It demands a ruling, but judges can delay, deny, ignore, or strike it. Use motions for compulsion, never for preservation.

Rule 3: A Praecipe preserves procedural integrity by bypassing judicial discretion.

Clerks must act on praecipes for writs, entries, corrections, and ministerial duties. Praecipes maintain the machinery of the case when judges obstruct.

Rule 4: A Judicial Notice is the Pro Se litigant's indestructible foundation.

It cannot be purged, cannot be silenced, and survives suppression. Even if ignored, it becomes mandatory reading for the appellate court.

Rule 5: Judicial Notice converts what the court avoids into what the record contains.

Blocked evidence, ignored objections, ex parte conduct, altered transcripts, missing docket entries, and refusals to rule all become preserved truth once noticed.

Rule 6: Judicial Notice neutralizes procedural sabotage.

If a Motion is struck, a Notice of Stricken Motion restores the evidence, exposes the strike itself, and protects your appeal. Silence becomes confession.

Rule 7: Judicial Notice is the substrate of every Documentation Weapon.

Footnotes point to it, Visual Law summarizes it, Exhibits anchor to it. Notice → Table → Exhibit Summary creates the evidentiary lattice no judge can escape.

Tactical Applications

- **Use motions to compel action, praecipes to enforce clerk duties, and Judicial Notices to preserve truth.**
  Each tool targets a different actor; using all three collapses their ability to evade.
- **When a motion is struck or ignored, immediately file "Judicial Notice of Stricken Motion" to restore the evidence and document the suppression.**
  This turns sabotage into appellate ammunition.
- **Preserve every procedural irregularity through Judicial Notice—blocked evidence,**

missing docket entries, altered transcripts, delays, refusals to rule, or ex parte conduct. What the court avoids becomes what the record contains.

- **Integrate Judicial Notice into all Documentation Weapons: Notice → Table → Exhibit Summary.**
Footnotes point to it; Visual Law displays it; Exhibits anchor to it.
This trinity forms an evidentiary lattice no judge can escape.

- **Keep every Judicial Notice to one verified page: cite the rule, state the fact, reference the exhibit, sign, and stop.**
Quiet filings survive; bloated ones give the court room to maneuver.

Rule of War

Motions can be denied.
Exhibits can be ignored.
Praecipes can be delayed.
But a Judicial Notice endures.

It is the Pro Se warrior's anchor —
the part of the record no judge can bury.

"Be nothing solicitous; but in every thing,
by prayer and supplication with thanksgiving,
let your requests be made known to God."
— Philippians 4:6

Chapter 45 – Doctrine Triad III—Footnotes · Visual Law · Exhibits

(The Documentation Weapons)

Footnotes (The Hidden Blade)

"For the commandment is a lamp, and the law a light, and reproofs of instruction are the way of life."
— Proverbs 6:23
(Truth beneath the line cuts deeper than argument above it.)

Visual Law (Truth Made Plain)

"Write the vision, and make it plain upon tables: that he that readeth it may run."
— Habakkuk 2:2
(Clarity forces the court to see what it would rather skim.)

Exhibits (Truth Curated and Lethal)

"Come now, and let us reason together, saith the Lord."
— Isaiah 1:18
(One excerpt properly framed is deadlier than a hundred pages scattered.)

BLUF (Bottom Line Up Front):

Documentation wins battles that argument cannot.
Footnotes shape understanding.
Visual Law shapes perception.
Exhibits shape what becomes real in the record.
Master these three weapons, and you control what the court sees—and therefore what it can lawfully decide.

Triad Doctrine

Footnotes whisper truth directly into the judge's ear.
Visual Law collapses complexity into clarity the court cannot avoid.
Exhibits curate the battlefield, isolating only what matters and discarding the noise.

These three weapons operate together:

- Footnotes **anchor the law and the logic**.
- Visual Law **forces decision**.
- Exhibits **lock the ruling into the record**.

They are not accessories.
They are the **attention weapons** of PSLW—the tools that reshape the court's field of vision.

Appellate judges rely more on documentation than argument; the triad is engineered for the eyes that will ultimately decide your case.

Rules of the Doctrine (Triad III)

Rule 1: Footnotes carry the law where argument cannot.

Above the line is persuasion; below the line is authority. Judges follow the authority.

Rule 2: Visual Law collapses ambiguity into decision.

When truth is displayed plainly, the court cannot retreat into narrative or noise.

Rule 3: Exhibits define reality for the court.

Judges rule based on what you isolate, not on what exists in the chaos of the case.

Rule 4: Documentation determines perception.

Those who control what the court sees control what the court can lawfully decide.

Rule 5: The Triad operates as a single weapon.

Footnotes anchor, Visual Law clarifies, Exhibits compel. Together, they build the record the court cannot escape.

Rule of War (Triad III):

*Guide the court's eyes, and you guide the outcome.
Control the footnote, the table, and the exhibit —
and you control the record.*

"For nothing is secret, that shall not be made manifest; nor hidden, that shall not be known and come to light."
— Luke 8:17

Chapter 46 – Doctrine of Footnotes as Weapons

"For the commandment is a lamp, and the law a light, and reproofs of instruction are the way of life."
— Proverbs 6:23

BLUF (Bottom Line Up Front)

Footnotes are not decoration. They are weapons.
A single properly crafted footnote can carry more force than three pages of argument because clerks and judges read footnotes as whispered confessions of truth—the part of a brief where litigants hide nothing and precision replaces persuasion.

Write footnotes as if you are speaking directly into the judge's ear.

The Doctrine

The Bluebook's *Bluepages* (B1–B21) were designed for practitioners and clerks, not academics. Courts recognize this cadence instantly: citation structure, typeface, short-form rules, and reporter abbreviations create an unmistakable visual signature of competence. When your filings match the court's internal language, your arguments carry weight beyond your status as Pro Se.

But footnotes do far more than signal professionalism.

Footnotes are where you place the weapons that win quietly: controlling law, procedural triggers, evidentiary precision, and facts so sharp the court cannot openly confront them without ruling in your favor.

Footnotes allow you to:

- correct a judge without embarrassing him,
- expose counsel's misquotations without drama,
- insert controlling law the court hoped to avoid,
- preserve appellate issues invisibly,
- and land precise pincites and parentheticals that force judicial recognition.

Footnotes are where truth speaks softly—and wins loudly.

Rules of the Doctrine

Rule 1: Footnotes are where authority lives.

Above the line persuades; below the line commands. Judges follow the command.

Rule 2: Precision is power.

One accurate pincite outweighs pages of unsourced argument.

Rule 3: Parentheticals sharpen the blade.

Seven to twelve words can quietly accomplish what paragraphs cannot.

Rule 4: Professional cadence builds judicial credibility.

Bluepages format subconsciously signals competence, discipline, and trustworthiness.

Rule 5: PDFs are the only safe ground.

If you cannot attach the official PDF, you cannot swear to the citation.

Rule 6: Footnotes are quiet correction.

Use them to expose misquotes, misstatements, and fabricated "rules" without provoking hostility.

Rule 7: Footnotes begin the appeal.

What is preserved below the line becomes ammunition above it.

Tactical Applications

1. Follow the Bluepages—Not the Academic Bluebook

Use the Bluepages rules for real litigation filings. They govern:

- case format
- short forms
- signals ("see," "cf.," "accord")

- reporter abbreviations
- punctuation and spacing

Courts expect this. Clerks respect this. Counsel fears this.

---

2. PDFs Are the Only Safe Source of Case Law

An official PDF of a court opinion is the complete, authenticated version of a court's opinion or order. It contains:

- full caption
- judge's signature block
- all pages, footnotes, dissents
- original emphasis
- appendices
- true pagination
- creation metadata

Anything else is not authoritative.

Commercial websites often provide truncated, altered, outdated, or editor-modified versions. These errors contaminate legal arguments. Only official PDFs guarantee accuracy.

Official sources:

- PACER / CM-ECF
- CourtListener (RECAP)
- GovInfo.gov
- State judiciary archives
- Clerk's Office certified copies

If you cannot attach the real PDF, you cannot rely on the case.

---

3. Use Pincites Ruthlessly

A pincite transforms a citation into evidence.

Weak:

> *West v. Atkins*, 487 U.S. 42 (1988).

Strong:

> *West v. Atkins*, 487 U.S. 42, 48–49 (1988).

Lethal:

> *West v. Atkins*, 487 U.S. 42, 48 (1988) (holding that a private physician under contract with the state acted under color of state law for purposes of 42 U.S.C. § 1983 because he was performing a function traditionally reserved to the state).

Pincites say: **"I read the law. You need to do the same."**

---

4. Parentheticals Are Surgical Blades

A single parenthetical can kill an argument:

- (reversing dismissal for lack of jurisdiction)
- (holding verified filings are evidence)
- (rejecting argument identical to opposing counsel's)

Parentheticals argue without arguing.

5. Paraphrase With Precision—Don't Overquote

Judges skip block quotes. Lawyers hide inside them.
You paraphrase to win; you quote only to kill.

---

6. Verify Every Citation Yourself

Never rely on Westlaw summaries, Lexis headnotes, Google Scholar excerpts, or attorney folklore.

Verification ends disputes instantly.

---

7. Stand on Your Briefs

When counsel invents law, simply write:

> *See Exhibit x (official court opinion PDF), demonstrating that counsel's proposed rule does not exist.*

No emotion, no combat—just death by evidence.

---

8. Whisper Through the Footnotes

Footnotes quietly:

- correct judicial misunderstanding,
- expose attorney deception,
- highlight statutory conflicts,
- connect facts without provoking bias.

Judges pretend not to read footnotes.
They read them first.

9. Use a Table of Authorities (TOA)

A TOA:

- proves mastery of the case
- guides the judge
- maps the appeal
- ensures citation integrity

Generate it after all footnotes are inserted.

---

10. Never Use "Passim"

Passim is a Latin term meaning **"scattered throughout."** In citations, it signals that a point appears "in many places" in the opinion or source—but the writer is unwilling (or unable) to identify *where*.

Judges and clerks interpret **passim** as:

- *I didn't read the case carefully.*
- *I don't know where the rule actually is.*
- *Somewhere in here, maybe, the court said something helpful.*
- *Please do my work for me.*

In modern litigation, **passim is a red flag** that the writer either:

- does not understand the authority,
- cannot locate a supporting passage, or
- is trying to inflate a weak argument.

It destroys credibility instantly.

Precision wins. Vagueness loses.
A single accurate pincite shows mastery.
"Passim" shows nothing.

"Passim" signals vagueness and intellectual laziness.
Precision wins.

Rule of War

The battle is won in the footnotes.
Whisper truth beneath the text,
and the court will hear you even when it pretends not to.

"For nothing is secret that shall not be made manifest;
nor hidden that shall not be known and come to light."
— Luke 8:17

Chapter 47 – Doctrine of Visual Law

"Write the vision, and make it plain upon tables: that he that readeth it may run."
— Habakkuk 2:2

BLUF (Bottom Line Up Front)

Most judges, clerks, and attorneys will never read your entire filing.
Some will not read a single paragraph before the hearing.
Visual Law—tables, charts, and binary decision matrices—forces them to see what they would otherwise avoid.
A well-crafted table can win a hearing before the first word is spoken.

Visual Law is not a stylistic choice. It is the price of survival in a system that only sees what you force it to see.

The Doctrine

Courts drown in paper.
Lawyers bury truth in text.
Clerks triage filings at high speed.
Judges skim for anchors, not prose.

After five years of high-intensity litigation, one truth stands above the rest:

If the court cannot see your argument in five seconds, it does not exist.

Visual Law exists because **brains read patterns, not paragraphs**.
A simple two-column table can do what twenty pages of briefing cannot:

- expose contradictions,
- eliminate ambiguity,
- force the court into a binary choice,
- and make misrepresentations impossible to justify.

When you place law, fact, evidence, and contradiction in a table with footnotes to the official PDFs, the court is compelled to follow your structure—not opposing counsel's chaos.

Visual Law is not decoration.
It is a control system for the court's attention.

Visual Law is also the native language of AI; when your tables are structured, AI analysis becomes perfect, and human error becomes impossible to hide.

Rules of the Doctrine

Rule 1: Visual Law is not optional—it is survival.

A court that cannot see your argument cannot rule lawfully on it. Visual Law forces recognition in a system that ignores what it cannot immediately grasp.

Rule 2: A Visual Law table must be understood in five seconds.

If your table does not deliver clarity in five seconds, it is not Visual Law—it is noise. The court decides based on what it can absorb instantly.

Rule 3: Binary structures destroy judicial ambiguity.

"Yes/No," "Lawful/Unlawful," "Admitted/Denied," "Within/Outside Jurisdiction."
Binary matrices remove escape hatches and force judges into legally binding outcomes.

Rule 4: Tables control attention—and attention controls rulings.

Judges skim. Clerks skim. Opposing counsel misdirects. Visual Law breaks through cognitive laziness and focuses the court where you need it.

Rule 5: Truth displayed plainly cannot be ignored or distorted.

A contradiction shown in a table is stronger than a contradiction described in prose. Visual Law closes the door on narrative manipulation.

Rule 6: Visual Law writes for the appellate court, not the trial judge.

Appellate judges rely on documentation, not oral argument. Tables become the blueprint for appellate review and often the spine of the final opinion.

When your Visual Law matrix cites Judicial Notices and official PDFs, the entire structure becomes appeal-proof.

Rule 7: Visual Law and AI operate in perfect alliance.

AI reads tables with near-perfect accuracy.
When you present law + fact + evidence in a structured grid, both human and machine are forced into the same coherent interpretation.

Rule 8: Visual Law is the quiet exposure of misconduct.

A table comparing "What the law requires" to "What the court did" demonstrates bias, delay, or suppression without ever using the words. The record—not you—makes the accusation.

Rule 9: The table is the Procedural Guillotine made visible.

When a Visual Law matrix shows unrebutted facts, missed deadlines, or statutory violations, the blade is already set. The court's ruling merely confirms gravity.

Tactical Applications

1. Compress the Entire Filing Into One Table

Every serious filing should contain at least one table that condenses your argument into a single, navigable grid.

Examples:
• **Issue → Law → Fact → Evidence (PDF) → Remedy**
• **Claim → Opposing Position → Verified Record → Citation**
• **Timeline → Actor → Document → Impact**

A table is a *procedural cage* into which you place the court.

---

2. Build Binary Decision Matrices

Judges hate ambiguity.
Tables that force **"Yes/No," "Allowed/Prohibited," "Admitted/Denied," "Within/Outside Jurisdiction"** leave no escape.

Binary matrices weaponize clarity.

Format:
Action | Source of Law | Court's Duty | Is It Met? (Yes/No)

When the final column shows the judge their own failure, the necessary ruling becomes obvious—or appealable.

---

3. Use Visual Law Because Judges Do Not Read Your Entire Filing

After hundreds of filings, hearings, and appeals, the pattern is undeniable:

- **Most judges skim.**

- **Most clerks skim.**
- **Many do not read a word before the hearing begins.**
- **Opposing counsel relies on this.**

Tables break through cognitive laziness.

Before a hearing, the clerk will often print *only the tables* or highlight them on screen.
During a hearing, judges turn to tables for reference.
During opinion drafting, a table becomes the outline for the judge's order.

Visual Law is how you **write the order for the judge**.

---

4. Cite in Footnotes—Not in the Table

Tables should be visually clean.
Citations should *anchor* facts, not clutter the visual field.

Use superscript footnotes in the table cells, with:

- pincites,
- parentheticals,
- and the official PDF used for verification.

This makes your table authoritative and unassailable.

---

5. Tables Are Silent Cross-Examination

A table forces opposing counsel to answer the structure you built:

- “Counsel, can you point to anything in Column 3 that supports your claim?”
- “Your Honor, Column 5 cites the official PDF contradicting their argument.”
- “As shown in Row 4, the statutory requirement is ‘shall,’ and the record is empty.”

A table turns the courtroom into a written cross-examination of the opposing lawyer.

They cannot escape it.
They cannot spin it.
They cannot hide.

---

6. Use Tables to Prove Judicial Misconduct Without Saying the Words

Visual Law lets you expose bias, suppression, delays, docket manipulation, or ultra vires actions **without making accusations**.

Example table:
Requirement (law) → What court did → Record citation → Lawful/Not Lawful

Placed in a motion or judicial notice, this forces a judge to either correct themselves or create a clean reversible error for appeal.

Visual Law is a mirror.
Judges see themselves in it.

Illustrative Table 1 – Binary Decision Matrix

(For demonstrating how a judge is forced into a Yes/No ruling based on law + record.)

Binary Decision Matrix (Example)

Action Required by Law	Controlling Authority	Record Evidence (Verified)	Court's Duty	Met? (Yes/No)
Court must rule on a timely filed motion within statutory period.	Rule 208.2(d)[1]	Timestamped filing & docket entry showing timely submission.	Issue a ruling or explain non-action on record.	**No**
Opposing party must rebut verified factual averments with specific denials.	Pa.R.C.P. 1029(b)[2]	Opposing filing contains only "denied as stated" without citing evidence.	Treat unrebutted facts as **admitted** by operation of law.	**No**

Notes

[1] *Parenthetical:* (requiring the court to dispose of motions within prescribed time).

[2] *Parenthetical:* (denials lacking specificity or evidence are deemed admissions).

Illustrative Table 2 – Issue → Law → Fact → Evidence → Remedy

(For demonstrating Visual Law compression of an entire filing into a single navigable grid.)

Issue–Law–Fact–Evidence–Remedy Table (Example)

Issue	Controlling Law	Verified Fact	Supporting Evidence (PDF)	Requested Remedy
Whether the filing was timely.	42 Pa.C.S. § 5571(a)[1]	Filing made on Day 29 of 30-day period.	Official PDF timestamp from ECF/PACER.[2]	Declare filing timely; proceed to merits.
Whether opposing counsel misquoted controlling authority.	Pa.R.P.C. 3.3(a)(1)[3]	Quoted text does not appear anywhere in the opinion.	Official court-issued PDF showing actual language.[4]	Strike misquotation; sanction or admonish as appropriate.

Notes

[1] *Parenthetical:* (appeals must be filed within 30 days unless statute tolls).

[2] *Parenthetical:* (timestamp in official docket PDF is controlling).

[3] *Parenthetical:* (attorney shall not knowingly make false statements of law).

[4] *Parenthetical:* (verified PDF demonstrates misquotation).

7. Create "Hearing Cards" for Oral Combat

Before a hearing, condense your strongest table onto a half-page card:

- Issue
- Law
- Fact
- Evidence (PDF)
- Remedy

This is your **spoken BLUF** in physical form.

Judges appreciate litigants who bring clarity.
Opposing counsel hates it.
You will walk into hearings more armed than any lawyer in the room.

---

8. Use Charts for Pattern Recognition

Charts (timelines, flow diagrams, metadata maps) reveal what narrative text hides.

Ideal chart types:

- **Timeline charts** (date → actor → action → exhibit → impact)
- **Metadata charts** (file hash → timestamp → chain of custody)
- **Fraud pattern charts** (claim → evidence → contradiction → relief)

Charts make deception visible.
Courts respond to what they can *see*.

9. Tables Win Appeals Before They Begin

Appellate clerks love tables.
They:

- map the issue,
- shorten research,
- remove noise,
- and highlight reversible error.

Your table becomes the appellate court's *scaffold* for its opinion.

Visual Law writes for the level above the judge in the room.

Rule of War

Words may be ignored.
Tables cannot.
Visual Law forces the court to confront the truth it tries not to see.

"For God is not the author of confusion,
but of peace."
— 1 Corinthians 14:33

Chapter 48 – Doctrine of Exhibits

"Come now, and let us reason together, saith the Lord."
— Isaiah 1:18

BLUF (Bottom Line Up Front)

Most exhibits are a waste of time, paper, and credibility.
Judges do not read them. Clerks do not flip through them.
Opposing lawyers weaponize them against you.
Your job is not to bury the court in paper—it is to **curate the battlefield**.
A perfect exhibit is short, numbered, excerpted, and lethal.

Appellate courts rely far more on exhibits than trial courts do—but only if those exhibits are excerpted, curated, and anchored.

The Doctrine

In five years of Pro Se and high-intensity litigation, one reality has become indisputable:

Judges and clerks rarely read your briefs—they will NEVER read your exhibits.

They will not dig through:

- 200 pages of screenshots,
- photo dumps,
- giant PDFs of irrelevant documents,
- transcripts,
- or "context packets."

Ninety percent of what Pro Se litigants submit as exhibits is **ignored**, **annoys the court**, or **buries the point** they needed to highlight.

Exhibits are not evidence dumps.
They are **precision kill shots**.
The purpose of an exhibit is to:

- isolate the one fact,
- anchor it to the record,
- control what the court sees,
- and make the ruling you want easy.

This doctrine teaches you how to **weaponize exhibits**—not drown the court with them.

Rules of the Doctrine:

Rule 1: An exhibit is not evidence unless the judge actually sees it.

Your job is to make seeing unavoidable.

Rule 2: Exhibits must isolate—not expand—the battlefield.

The fewer pages, the stronger the blow.

Exhibits obey the same law as filings: the fewer pages you use, the more force each page carries.

Rule 3: Summary pages are the exhibit; the attachment is optional.

Judges rule on the summary, not the stack behind it.

Where possible, summary pages should also reference the docket number from which the excerpt originates.

Rule 4: A docket-anchored citation is stronger than a 200-page attachment.

The court trusts its own record more than your PDF.

Rule 5: Every exhibit must carry a single purpose: to compel the ruling you want.

If it doesn't, cut it.

Rule 6: Exhibits operate as Visual Law.

Truth made visible always defeats truth buried in text.

Rule 7: Exhibits write for appeal, not the trial court.

Appellate judges rely on what is excerpted, cited, and curated—not dumped.

Tactical Applications

1. Never Use Exhibits to "Show Everything"

Exhibits are not storage containers. They are scalpels. Every exhibit must answer one question:

"Does this move the court toward the ruling I want?"

If the answer is no, delete it.

2. Always Number Exhibits—Never Letter Them

Use numbering systems, not alphabetical labels:

Exhibit 1, 1.1, 1.2, 1.3
Exhibit 2, 2.1, 2.2

Numbering:

- reinforces hierarchy,
- prevents clerical misfiling,
- accommodates large multi-part exhibits,
- and psychologically signals "organized, professional, credible."

Letters (A, B, C...) and sub-letters (A-1, A-2...) scream **Pro Se** and are easily mis-sorted by clerks and e-filing systems.

---

3. Every Exhibit Needs a Summary Page Up Front

The first page of **every** exhibit must be:

Exhibit 1.1 – Summary of Key Excerpts
Exhibit 1.2 – Summary of Controlling Language

On that first page provide:

- the exact snippet or passage used,
- a one-sentence takeaway,

- pincites or line references,
- and the official PDF citation.

This ensures the judge and clerk **see what you want them to see**, not the garbage around it.

---

4. Use Docket Anchoring—the Most Powerful Exhibit Technique

Whenever possible, instead of attaching the full document, do this:

"See Docket No. 27 at 3–4 (official PDF)."

This forces the court to look at:

- its **own** record,
- its **own** timestamps,
- and its **own** filings.

Docket anchoring:

- makes fabrication impossible,
- prevents clerks from claiming confusion,
- avoids huge file sizes,
- and gives your exhibit **judicial authority**.

This is how you make the docket fight for you.

---

5. Only Attach Full Documents When Required

Full attachments should be rare. Limit to:

- judicial opinions,
- orders,
- certified transcripts,
- government records explicitly required by rule.

Everything else should be excerpted.

A 150-page exhibit is not evidence—it is a **garbage dump**.

---

6. Excerpt Transcripts—Never Attach Full Transcripts

Never include full transcripts unless they are **not already in the docket**, and only then attach them as the **last exhibit** in your set. Full transcripts bury your critical exhibits, inflate the record, and guarantee that neither the judge nor the clerk will read anything beyond them. If a transcript already exists in the docket, **never reattach it**—instead, excerpt only the exact lines you need and cite the docket number (e.g., "Docket No. 47, at 41:17–42:9"). Excerpts go up front; full transcripts go last, if ever.

Transcripts are:

- curated,
- manipulated,
- quietly edited,
- often incomplete,
- and designed to make Pro Se litigants look incoherent.

Full transcripts clog the record and bury your arguments.

Instead:

- pull **only the necessary lines,**
- mark them with line numbers,
- identify speaker,
- and include them as **Exhibit X.1 (Transcript Excerpts).**

If the transcript is already in the docket, do NOT reattach it.
Anchor it:

> *"See Transcript, Docket No. 62, at 41:17–42:9."*

That single line has more power than a 500-page PDF.

---

7. Exhibit Summaries Control the Hearing

Judges often flip directly to your exhibits during hearing.
So the summary page **becomes your oral argument.**

It is your BLUF in physical form.
It is the roadmap the judge will use when drafting the order.

Your job:
Prepare the exhibit they will actually read—not the one you wish they had read.

---

8. Exhibits Should Be Fewer Than 10% of Total Pages

A filing with:

- 20 pages argument + 200 pages exhibits = **ignored.**
  A filing with:

- 20 pages argument + 8 pages exhibits = **readable**.

Minimalism wins.

---

9. Exhibits Are Visual Law—Not Dump Law

An exhibit is another form of **Visual Law**:

- compressed,
- curated,
- page-first,
- and designed for skimming.

Your extract page should look like a mini-table or mini-matrix.

When clerks see your exhibit summary, they think:
"Thank you. This is usable."

Appellate judges do not review bulk—they review clarity. Exhibits must speak cleanly for themselves.

---

10. Exhibits Create Instant Appellate Value

Appellate courts love exhibits that:

- are excerpted,
- cite official PDFs,
- point to docket numbers,
- highlight contradictions,
- and include controlled summaries.

When the trial judge ignores your exhibit, the appellate panel sees the **clean reversible error** immediately.

Illustrative Exhibit Format (Drop-In Example)

Exhibit 3.1—Summary of Key Excerpts (Official PDF Attached as 3.2)

- *Statutory Requirement:* "The court **shall** rule within 20 days."
- *PDF Citation:* 42 Pa.C.S. § 1234(a) (official PDF, at 7).
- *Verified Fact:* No ruling by Day 45.
- *Takeaway:* Mandatory deadline violated; relief required.

Exhibit 3.2—Official PDF (Pages 6–9 Excerpted)
(Place only necessary pages; highlight relevant language; include pincites.)

Rule of War

Exhibits do not convince the court—summary pages do. Control what they see, and you control what they can rule.

"Prove all things; hold fast that which is good."
— 1 Thessalonians 5:21

Chapter 49 – Doctrine of Docket Integrity

"A false balance is an abomination before the Lord: but a just weight is his will." (Prov. 11:1)

BLUF (Bottom Line Up Front):

Courts live and die by the integrity of their dockets. Judges, attorneys, and clerks exploit this system routinely with backdating, suppression, and tactical misfiling. But when a Pro Se litigant documents the manipulation, they cry "vexatious" or "frivolous." The Docket Integrity Doctrine turns this double standard into a weapon: exposing that the only party preserving integrity is the Pro Se, while the professionals sabotage it.

The Doctrine

Docket Integrity is not about catching corruption—it is about proving structure.
Courts expect Pro Se litigants to rely on memory; PSLW relies on metadata, timestamps, and verified notices.
When the docket becomes the battlefield, integrity becomes your shield and documentation becomes your sword.

The Nature of Docket Manipulation

- **Clerical Weaponization:** Prothonotaries "lose" filings, delay docketing, or misclassify motions to blunt their impact.
- **Judicial Backdating:** Orders created days later are dated retroactively to make Pro Se filings look untimely. Metadata proves the lie.
- **Holiday Gambits:** Orders filed Friday afternoons or before holidays, designed to steal days from your response window.
- **Transcript Curation:** Court reporters and staff sanitize transcripts to erase threats, admissions, or misconduct.

These are not rare accidents. They are routine survival tactics by a system that resents exposure.

Why They Fear Pro Se Record–Building

Attorneys and judges expect litigants to argue feelings, not facts. When a Pro Se litigant:

- Checks metadata,
- Cross–references transcript vs. audio,
- Files Judicial Notices of docket suppression,
- Creates annotated timelines,

...it terrifies the insiders. Because once documented, their games become visible and appealable.

That is why the same actors who casually tamper with the docket will accuse you of "harassment" for filing Notices of Preservation. They are not defending the law—they are defending their monopoly on misconduct.

Rules of the Doctrine

Rule 1: Assume every docket is tampered.

Trust nothing unless you downloaded it yourself, timestamped it, and preserved the metadata.

Metadata is objective evidence; the court cannot explain it away.

Rule 2: Document the manipulation, not the motive.

Do not scream corruption—show timestamps, filing confirmations, missing notices. Let the record accuse.

Rule 3: File the Pair. For every irregularity, file:

- **Judicial Notice** – preservation of the defect.
- **Motion** – compels the court to either strike, rule, or deny (appealable).

Rule 4: Turn Delay Into Confession.

If the court fails to rule, the record shows suppression, not silence. Judicial inaction becomes your evidence.

Rule 5: Never Let Them Define You.

When they cry “frivolous” or “vexatious,” remember: the real vexation is their docket tampering. Your role is not noise, but preservation.

Why This Works

The appellate system only sees the record. If the record shows:

- You filed clean, verified Notices and Motions;
- They responded with delay, suppression, or silence;
- You preserved every irregularity with metadata, timestamps, and confirmation logs–

then the higher court cannot ignore the imbalance. Even hostile panels know: the system collapses if docket integrity is openly compromised.

Appellate judges cannot ignore docket irregularities that are documented with precision; they must explain or correct them.

Strategic Posture

You are not fighting to “prove” misconduct. You are documenting it so thoroughly that their denials become absurd.

Your filings should read like a logbook:

- Date, time, docket stamp, PDF creation date.
- Service notices missing.

- Entries posted late or backdated.

Every discrepancy becomes a blade.

Rule of War:

The docket is the battlefield. *They will weaponize it. You must defend it. The Docket Integrity Doctrine means you never fight on their terms—you force every manipulation into the light, where it becomes their confession.*

"Providing good things not only in the sight of God, but also in the sight of all men." (2 Cor. 8:21)

Chapter 50 – Doctrine of Counter–Manipulation

"The wise man is strong: and a knowing man, stout and valiant." (Prov. 24:5)

BLUF (Bottom Line Up Front):

Corrupt judges, clerks, and attorneys rely on procedural gamesmanship—docket suppression, backdating, delayed notices, curated transcripts—to tilt the field. The **Counter–Manipulation Doctrine** flips those tactics into appellate ammunition.

You do not just survive their tricks; you weaponize them—and turn every irregularity into a procedural confession the appellate court cannot ignore.

Counter–Manipulation is not about alleging misconduct—it is about documenting structure with such precision that misconduct reveals itself.

The Reality of Manipulation

- **Clerical Suppression:** Filings "lost," misclassified, or delayed to kill momentum.
- **Backdating Orders:** PDF creation dates never match the docket stamp, but are used to make your filings appear late.
- **Holiday Gambits:** Orders or writs filed just before weekends or holidays, stealing 3–5 days off your clock.
- **Transcript Curation:** Court reporters sanitize transcripts to remove threats, admissions, or misconduct.
- **Silence as Denial:** Judges refuse to rule, hoping your filings expire in limbo.

These are not accidents. They are systemic tactics meant to exhaust Pro Se litigants into silence.

The Doctrine

Courts and attorneys expect Pro Se litigants to fight on emotional terrain.

Counter–Manipulation shifts the battlefield to structural terrain—timestamps, metadata, service logs, docket sequencing, and verified notices that cannot be argued with and cannot be dismissed without consequence.

The system's games rely on one assumption:
that you will not notice, will not understand, or will not document the manipulation.

PSLW doctrines shatter that assumption.

Counter–Manipulation reframes every irregularity as procedural evidence—not moral accusation.
You do not try to stop their tactics; you turn their tactics into appellate fuel.

When they delay, you create a timeline.
When they backdate, you expose the metadata.
When they suppress filings, you document the denial.
When they curate transcripts, you anchor the audio.
When they refuse to rule, you convert silence into constructive denial.

Your goal is not to prove corruption—that is the trap they want you to fall into.

Your goal is to **document inconsistency so cleanly that the appellate court must reverse or explain, and neither option favors the trial court.**

Counter–Manipulation applies a simple principle:
Every procedural violation is an opportunity.
Every discrepancy is a blade.
Every silence is a corner.
Every backdated order is a confession in the metadata.

Institutional actors are not afraid of your arguments.
They are afraid that you will show the next court—and the next—the paper trail they hoped no one would ever trace.

Counter–Manipulation makes that trail impossible to hide.

Rules of the Doctrine

Rule 1: Assume manipulation is constant.

Every docket, order, and transcript is suspect until you verify it.

Rule 2: Document, do not accuse.

Avoid adjectives like "corrupt." Instead, show:

- Docket entry timestamp vs. PDF metadata creation date.
- Service confirmations missing.
- Docket entries unmade or removed.
- Orders appearing days late.

Metadata has no motive; it cannot be coached, curated, or intimidated.

Let the evidence accuse.

Rule 3: File in Pairs. For every irregularity, file both:

- **Judicial Notice** – preserves the defect.
- **Motion** – compels a ruling.
  This creates two appellate hooks: one if ignored (constructive denial), one if denied (appealable ruling).

Rule 4: Turn Delay Into Confession.

Judicial silence is not absence—it is suppression. File a notice of preservation when deadlines expire without rulings. Delay becomes your exhibit on appeal.

Rule 5: Make Manipulation Their Problem.

When you expose suppression, backdating, or silence with precision, higher courts are forced to confront that the trial court is not merely biased—it is procedurally illegitimate.

Why This Terrifies Them

Attorneys and judges expect you to argue feelings. They are unprepared when you:

- Pull metadata,
- Compare transcript against audio,
- File preservation notices with timestamps and service records,
- Create annotated timelines.

When you do, their games become visible, appealable, and undeniable.

A Visual Law table comparing docket timestamps to PDF metadata is the fastest way to expose manipulation without saying the word.

Why This Works

Appellate courts live on paper. They do not hear your outrage; they read your record. If your record shows:

- You filed clean, verified motions,
- Judges and clerks responded with suppression, silence, or backdated entries,

- You documented every step with timestamps and confirmation numbers,

...then even hostile appellate judges are boxed in. To rule against you, they must bless open docket manipulation—something they cannot do without destroying their own legitimacy.

Strategic Posture

You are not trying to stop docket manipulation. You are turning it into your weapon.

- Their **delay** becomes your **appeal exhibit**.
- Their **backdating** becomes your **metadata proof of fraud**.
- Their **silence** becomes your **constructive denial**.
- Their **curated transcript** becomes your **audio–transcript mismatch filing**.

Rule of War:

Procedural gamesmanship is not your enemy—it is your raw material. The Counter–Manipulation Doctrine means every trick they play becomes another blade in your arsenal, forged into appellate ammunition.

"That we be not overreached by Satan. For we are not ignorant of his devices." (2 Cor. 2:11)

Chapter 51 – Doctrine of Procedural Mirror

"With the pure thou wilt be pure: and with the perverse thou wilt be perverted."
— 2 Samuel 22:27

BLUF (Bottom Line Up Front):

Every time the court or opposing counsel bends procedure—by backdating, suppressing, delaying, or misfiling—you mirror it back. The Doctrine of Procedural Mirror means you do not fight corruption with outrage. You fight it by reflecting their manipulation back into the record so precisely that it becomes your appellate weapon.

The Doctrine

Procedural Mirror turns every act of manipulation into evidence by reflecting it back into the record with timestamps, metadata, and verified filings.
You do not accuse the court—you let the court's own actions accuse itself.
By documenting each irregularity rather than reacting to it, you convert backdating into metadata variance, suppression into preserved notice, delay into constructive denial, and

transcript curation into audio contradiction.
The mirror shifts the battle from emotion to structure: you reflect precisely what they did, and the appellate court sees the truth they hoped to hide.

The Nature of the Mirror

- **They hide filings → You file proof of missing notices.**
- **They backdate orders → You file metadata showing the creation date.**
- **They suppress motions → You file Judicial Notice of suppression with timestamps.**
- **They delay rulings → You file Motion to Compel or Notice of Constructive Denial.**
- **They curate transcripts → You file the audio comparison.**

The mirror shows them what they did—and makes sure the appellate court sees it too.

Why This Doctrine Matters

Judges and attorneys despise Pro Se litigants not because they are loud, but because they are accurate. When you reflect their procedural games back into the record, you destroy their plausible deniability. Silence, delay, and tampering stop being invisible.

Rules of the Doctrine

Rule 1: Record, Do not React.

When manipulation occurs, resist the urge to editorialize. Document it with timestamps, metadata, docket confirmations, and side–by–side comparisons.

Rule 2: Reflect, Do not Argue.

You are not accusing the judge of being corrupt—you are reflecting the record into the record. "The order is dated July 29 but created July 30 at 12:29 p.m." is unanswerable.

Rule 3: Pair Every Reflection.

For each irregularity:

- File a **Judicial Notice** to preserve it.
- File a **Motion** to compel action or strike.

Rule 4: Make the Mirror Procedural.

Never call it "fraud." Call it "procedural defect," "irregularity," or "suppression." Courts hate the language of corruption but cannot ignore the language of procedure.

Rule 5: Silence Is the Final Reflection.

If the court ignores your Motion, that silence itself becomes mirrored—a Notice of Constructive Denial that feeds directly into appeal.

Tactical Applications

- **Holiday Filing Trap:** They file on Friday to burn your days. → You file Judicial Notice of Holiday Filing to preserve the lost time.
- **Backdated Order:** PDF says created Aug 30, docket says Aug 28. → You file Judicial Notice of Metadata Variance and Motion to Strike.
- **Transcript Omission:** Your objection missing. → You file Judicial Notice of Transcript Variance with audio comparison.
- **Suppressed Filing:** Your emergency motion never docketed. → You file Judicial Notice of Docket Suppression, attach filing confirmation.

Each manipulation becomes its own confession.

Why It Works

Appellate courts are blind to feelings but sensitive to records. When your filings show exact procedural manipulations—and you mirrored them into the record with notices and motions—the higher court cannot unsee it.

The mirror makes corruption undeniable, without you ever using the word.

Rule of War:

When they twist the process, do not rage. Reflect. The Doctrine of Procedural Mirror ensures every act of manipulation bounces back into the record—sharper, cleaner, and ready for appellate review.

"To the weak I became weak, that I might gain the weak. I became all things to all men, that I might save all." (1 Cor. 9:22)

Chapter 52 – Doctrine of Exhaustion

"They that hope in the Lord shall renew their strength, they shall take wings as eagles." (Isaiah 40:31)

BLUF (Bottom Line Up Front):

Never run to the appellate court before you have pounded the trial court into the ground with verified filings, procedural traps, and preserved objections. The Doctrine of Exhaustion means you make the lower court choke on the record—so that on appeal, every silence, every irregularity, every manipulated order is already documented beyond denial.

The Doctrine

Exhaustion is disciplined procedural pressure, not repetition: you do not persuade the trial judge—you force the record to speak.

By documenting timestamps, metadata, unrebutted facts, silence, and sequencing, you shift the battle from emotion to structure.

Improper rulings become reversible error; refusal to rule becomes constructive denial; delay becomes procedural confession.

Exhaustion means you do not allege misconduct—you document the structure until the misconduct documents itself.

What Exhaustion Really Means

- **Not Just Administrative:** Lawyers teach exhaustion as "you have to appeal only after trying below." That is surface level.
- **True Exhaustion:** You do not just file once. You file until silence becomes confession. You hammer every procedural defect. You file motions, notices, verifications, and proposed orders until the court has either ruled (appealable) or refused (constructive denial).
- **Why:** If you skip this, appellate courts dismiss you with a shrug: *"Not preserved. Not exhausted."*

Why It Matters More Now Than Ever

- **AI & Technology:** Courts are moving toward AI-assisted review. That means it will not be a charming lawyer in oral argument that sways an outcome—it will be the written record.
- **Written Record Is Everything:** Metadata, timestamps, unrebutted notices—these are what AI

(and appellate clerks) will parse. The more disciplined your record, the stronger your appeal.

- **The Coming Shift:** As AI integrates, manipulation by lawyers ("weasel words" in oral arguments, lies without consequence) will carry less weight. What is written—what is verifiable—will dominate. That is your battlefield.

Why They Hate Exhaustion

- **You Flip the Power Dynamic:** Judges and lawyers are used to controlling outcomes with tone, influence, and bias. Exhaustion strips that away—it reduces them to clerks of the law, where they belong.
- **Exposure of the Status Quo:** They despise that you are not playing "pretend lawyer." You are an engineer applying their own rules against them—systematically, relentlessly, without theatrics.
- **It Robs Them of Discretion:** Discretion is their shield. Exhaustion removes it by boxing them into the law and record they cannot escape.

The Rules of the Doctrine

Rule 1: Pound the Trial Court First.

Never leave defects unchallenged. File motions to strike, vacate, compel, or notice of suppression. Do not appeal on a thin record.

Rule 2: Preserve Every Level.

- Trial Court: Objections and motions.
- Appellate Court: Motions for reconsideration, supplemental notices.
- Supreme Court/Federal: Cert petitions, constitutional hooks.

Rule 3: Make Silence Your Exhibit.

When they refuse to rule, file Notice of Constructive Denial. Exhaustion means showing you forced them to confess through silence.

Rule 4: Use Verification as Ammunition.

Verified filings are sworn statements. If unrebutted, they become judicial admissions. Pound the trial court with them.

Rule 5: Appeal Only on a Full Arsenal.

Never walk into appellate court saying "the trial judge was unfair." Walk in with 20 verified filings, 10 ignored motions, 5 backdated orders, and an audio variance. That is exhaustion.

Tactical Applications

- **Example 1:** You file a Motion to Vacate → ignored. File a Judicial Notice of Constructive Denial. File a Motion to Compel Ruling. File again with metadata proof. Now you have three layers of preservation before appeal.

- **Example 2:** An appellate panel once dismissed for "waiver" until shown ten ignored trial–level motions; the sheer volume of preserved silence forced reconsideration.
- **Result:** On appeal, you do not argue "bias." You show the exact procedural choke points where the trial court refused to act. The appellate panel has no escape route.

Why Exhaustion Wins

- **Appellate courts are allergic to noise, but addicted to clean records.**
- By exhausting every procedural avenue, you remove their ability to dismiss.
- Every denial becomes reversible. Every silence becomes confession. Every irregularity becomes evidence.

Rule of War:

Do not run. Do not skip. Do not beg the appellate court to fix what you failed to hammer below. ***Exhaust the trial court until its misconduct is undeniable. Then, and only then, take the corpse of that record to appeal.***

"Let us not be weary in doing good: for in due time we shall reap, not failing." (Gal. 6:9)

Chapter 53 – Doctrine of Appellate Exhaustion

"For the Lord is a God of judgment: blessed are all they that wait for him." (Isaiah 30:18)

BLUF (Bottom Line Up Front):

Appeals are not won in appellate court—they are won by exhausting every procedural avenue in the trial court and carrying that record upward. The Appellate Exhaustion Protocol is the filing pattern you execute *after judgment* to ensure that every issue is preserved, every silence is recorded, and every appellate trap is closed.

The Doctrine

Appellate Exhaustion shifts the battle from persuasion to preservation. The trial judge is no longer your audience—the appellate panel is. Your job is not to win below, but to **construct a record the appellate court cannot ignore and the trial court cannot survive**.

You achieve this by documenting structure, not emotion: timestamps, metadata, unrebutted notices, missing rulings, misdated orders, and suppressed filings.

Improper rulings become reversible error; refusal to rule becomes constructive denial; delay becomes procedural confession.

Appellate Exhaustion is not accusation—it is documentation so disciplined that the misconduct documents itself.

Why This Protocol Exists

- **Courts dismiss appeals not on merits, but on "waiver."** If you did not raise it below, they will not hear it above.
- **Trial judges weaponize delay.** They ignore motions hoping you will not preserve.
- **Appellate clerks look for shortcuts.** The easiest dismissal order is "issue not preserved."
- **Pro Se litigants lose appeals not because they are wrong, but because they left gaps in the record.**

This Protocol ensures there are no gaps.

Core Filing Pattern

1. Post–Judgment Motions (Trial Court)

- File **Motion to Vacate Judgment** (Pa.R.C.P. 227.1 or equivalent).
- File **Motion for Reconsideration** (Pa.R.A.P. 1701(b)(3) or equivalent).

- File **Motion to Correct or Modify Record** (Pa.R.A.P. 1926).
- Each motion is verified, served, and time–stamped.

2. Judicial Notice of Constructive Denial

- If motions are ignored past deadline, file Judicial Notice:
  "Defendant hereby preserves that the Court's failure to rule constitutes a constructive denial, preserved for appeal."

3. Parallel Notice of Appeal

- Do not wait. File a timely **Notice of Appeal** while post–judgment motions are pending.
- Pa.R.A.P. 1701(b)(3) allows trial courts to act on pending motions during appeal—preserve both tracks.

4. Supplemental Filings (Appellate Court)

- File **Application for Relief** under Pa.R.A.P. 123 when trial court fails to act.
- File **Supplemental Judicial Notice** attaching unrebutted trial–court motions and docket suppression evidence.
- File **Motion to Strike Opposing Brief** if it relies on facts outside record or misstates law.

5. Preservation of Federal Hooks

- Frame due process violations as federal claims: denial of hearing (5th/14th Amendments), suppression of filings (§1983), bias (Caperton v. Massey).

- Include in your appellate brief, even if not primary issue, to preserve SCOTUS jurisdiction.

Rules of the Doctrine

Rule 1: Double–File Every Time.

Motion (compel) + Judicial Notice (preserve). One forces action, the other boxes silence.

Rule 2: Time Is Everything.

File within hours, never days. Appellate deadlines are jurisdictional—miss them and you are done.

Rule 3: Redundancy Is Protection.

File in both trial and appellate courts when in doubt. Better to be repetitive than waived.

Rule 4: Federalize Early.

Always frame state–court misconduct as federal constitutional deprivation. This secures higher review.

Rule 5: Appeal Is Paper, Not Argument.

Oral argument rarely changes outcomes. Written record decides. Make yours unassailable.

Tactical Applications

- **Judge ignores motion for reconsideration:** File Judicial Notice of Constructive Denial + Application for Relief in appellate court.
- **Prothonotary suppresses docket entry:** Attach filing confirmation and USPS/email timestamp in appellate supplement.
- **Opposing counsel lies in brief:** File Motion to Strike, cite Pa.R.A.P. 123, attach proof of misrepresentation.
- **Trial court refuses transcript:** File Judicial Notice of Transcript Withholding + request under Pa.R.A.P. 1926 (correction of record).

Why This Works

- **It removes waiver.** Appellate courts cannot say you failed to preserve—you have documented every attempt.
- **It exposes bias.** Silence and delay become part of your appellate record.
- **It pressures opposing counsel.** They must respond to every redundant filing, multiplying their risk of error.
- **It positions you federally.** If state courts stonewall, the record screams due process denial for federal §1983 or habeas relief.

Rule of War:

Appeals are not mercy reviews—they are record audits. The Appellate Exhaustion Protocol ensures that when the higher court reads your record, they see a disciplined warrior who filed, preserved, and mirrored every defect. Waiver dies, and bias becomes evidence.

"Rejoicing in hope. Patient in tribulation. Instant in prayer." (Rom. 12:12)

Chapter 54 – Doctrine of How Judges and Lawyers See the Pro Se Litigant

---

"I am become a derision all the day, all scoff at me." (Jer. 20:7)

BLUF (Bottom Line Up Front):

The legal establishment does not view Pro Se litigants as equals in the courtroom. Judges see you as a burden, attorneys see you as a nuisance or a risk, and even well-intentioned "Pro Se reforms" have not moved the needle on outcomes. Understanding how they perceive you is essential—because only then can you weaponize their biases into appellate ammunition.

The Doctrine

Judges and lawyers do not see Pro Se litigants as equals—they see them as burdens, risks, and statistical non-factors. Their perception is not personal; it is structural. The legal system is built on assumptions of incompetence, emotional volatility, and procedural ignorance.

The Doctrine of How They See You is not about resentment—it is about **intel**.
Once you understand the lens through which the court views you, you stop expecting fairness and start building a record strong enough to overcome bias. Their assumptions become predictable patterns. Their patterns become procedural openings. And those openings become appellate weapons.

You do not fight the perception.
You **exploit** it—by behaving with more discipline, verification, and structure than the system expects or knows how to counter.

Rules of the Doctrine

Rule 1: Assume the "Pro Se Penalty" is real and immediate.

The label alone triggers lowered credibility, heightened scrutiny, and judicial impatience. Start every case knowing you begin in a hole—and doctrine is how you climb out.

Rule 2: Expect a double standard—and prepare for it.

Attorneys are forgiven for sloppiness; Pro Se litigants are punished for precision. This is not unfair—it is predictable. Treat it as terrain, not tragedy.

Rule 3: Replace assumed incompetence with undeniable structure.

Judges expect emotion. Lawyers expect confusion. You answer with verification, timestamps, Visual Law, and Judicial Notices. Structure demolishes stereotype.

Rule 4: Turn bias into procedural advantage.

When they underestimate you, they make mistakes: missed deadlines, unsupported assertions, sloppy citations, procedural shortcuts. Doctrine turns their contempt into evidence.

Rule 5: Their perception is an obstacle in the trial court and a weapon in the appellate court.

Bias at trial becomes reversible error on appeal—but only if you exhaust the lower court and preserve everything.

Rule 6: You do not seek their respect—you force their compliance.

Respect is irrelevant. Only rulings matter. Rulings are controlled by the record. The record is controlled by you.

Rule 7: The Pro Se advantage begins when you stop trying to fight the stereotype and start making it irrelevant.

You will not change how they see you. But you can change what the record reveals about them.

The Professional View of Pro Se

Attorneys are trained to treat Pro Se opponents as *different*—not in a good way.

- An **ABA guide for attorneys** warns that "courts will generally give self-represented litigants some leeway on procedural matters," making timely resolution difficult.
- Lawyers are advised to "document everything," avoid legal jargon, and always put communications in writing. This is not to help you—it is to protect *them* from you.
- Another bar publication bluntly tells lawyers: litigating against Pro Se "comes with risks," because Pro Se parties may swamp the docket with filings, appeal every adverse ruling, or even sue judges and opposing counsel.

In short: **you are not treated as an equal party, you are treated as a liability.**

Judicial Perceptions

Judges often start with skepticism before you even open your mouth.

- Empirical studies show that the **"Pro Se" label itself is a negative signal**. Judges and clerks assume you are less competent, less credible, and less prepared than an attorney.
- Richard Posner, one of the most respected federal appellate judges of the last generation, resigned from the Seventh Circuit in part because, in his words, his

colleagues "didn't like the Pro Se's and didn't want to do anything with them."

- Judges often give lip service to fairness but in practice will overlook rule violations for attorneys while punishing Pro Se parties for smaller missteps. This is the **double standard of discretion** your doctrines are designed to crush.
- To the judiciary, the Pro Se is not a litigant—he is a workload.

The Reality of Outcomes

The statistics are brutal:

- In federal district courts from 1998–2017, **Pro Se plaintiffs won only 3–4% of cases**, and **Pro Se defendants lost 80–90% of the time**.
- By comparison, when both parties are represented, plaintiffs and defendants each win about 50% of the time.
- **Court reforms do not help**. Help desks, handbooks, Pro Se clerks, and even entire "Pro Se offices" have been studied—and none improved outcomes in any measurable way.

This is why the **Doctrine of Exhaustion** is non-negotiable. You cannot expect the system to help you. You must build the record yourself, pound the trial court, and weaponize every irregularity.

The Fear of Lawyers

Even though they dismiss Pro Se litigants publicly, lawyers admit privately that you are dangerous if you know what you are doing.

- A professional liability defense article cautions that Pro Se parties "may be more likely to seek sanctions, appeal every ruling, or swamp the case with paper," turning straightforward matters into expensive nightmares.
- Another article warns that "Pro Se litigants are often emotionally invested and unable to assess their own case objectively"—but also acknowledges that **when you are disciplined, you are unpredictable and hard to control.**
- Lawyers are explicitly trained not to advise you, not to befriend you, and not to let their guard down around you. That is because they know that a well–prepared Pro Se can flip procedural errors into bar complaints, sanctions motions, or appeals.

What This Means for You

1. **You start from behind.** Judges assume incompetence. Attorneys assume weakness. The label "Pro Se" is itself a handicap.

2. **You will lose most of the time—unless you adopt doctrine.** The win rates (3–4%) prove that random self–representation fails.
3. **You terrify them when you are disciplined.** The very articles meant to train lawyers against you confirm that you can overwhelm them with paper, expose their misconduct, and force appeals.
4. **The reforms will not save you.** Help desks and pamphlets are window–dressing. They change perception, not outcomes.

Rule of War:

Know how they see you. *The judge thinks you are a nuisance. The attorney thinks you are a risk. The statistics say you are doomed. Only doctrine—relentless, verified, disciplined doctrine—flips the script. By reflecting their biases back into the record, you make their contempt into your appeal.*

"We are made as the refuse of this world, the offscouring of all even until now." (1 Cor. 4:13)

Chapter 55 – Doctrine of the Signaling Effect

"Set up a standard on the walls of Babylon, make the watch strong." (Jer. 51:12)

BLUF (Bottom Line Up Front):

The word *"Pro Se"* is not just a label—it is a stigma. Judges, clerks, and lawyers read it as incompetence, unreliability, and weakness. That signal tilts the field against you before you even speak. Your task is to flip the signal: to use discipline, precision, and record-building to turn contempt into evidence and bias into ammunition.

The Doctrine

The word *Pro Se* is not neutral—it is a signal. The moment a filing hits the docket with that label, judges and clerks subconsciously downgrade its credibility. That is the **legal signal**: Pro Se equals frivolous until proven otherwise. Inside courtroom culture, the label also functions as a **social signal**: Pro Se litigants are outsiders, disruptors of hierarchy, and presumed problems before they speak. And the data is unambiguous—the **empirical signal** confirms the bias: Pro Se plaintiffs win only 3–4% of cases, Pro Se defendants lose 80–90%, and decades of "reforms" have changed nothing.

The system reads your status before it reads your argument. The signal shapes the posture of the court long before the merits are reached. Doctrine exists so you can flip that signal—turning their presumption of incompetence into your first piece of appellate evidence.

Rules of the Doctrine

Rule 1: Accept the Handicap.

The stigma is real. Do not expect neutrality.

Rule 2: Flip the Signal With Discipline.

File short, verified, statute–anchored submissions. Surprise judges expecting chaos.

Rule 3: Mirror the Signal.

When ignored, mocked, or suppressed, file Judicial Notice. Turn their bias into record evidence.

Rule 4: Neutralize Emotion.

Do not confirm the stereotype. No rants, no clutter. Precision is your defiance.

Rule 5: Speak Clinically.

Own your status: *"Defendant, appearing Pro Se."* Say it flatly, without apology.

Tactical Applications

- **Accused of being frivolous:** File precise, verified motions with statutory cites. Each denial becomes proof of bias.
- **Ignored by the court:** File Judicial Notice of Constructive Denial. Silence becomes confession.
- **Mocked for being Pro Se:** Anchor in law, not emotion. Show competence instead of arguing status.
- **On appeal:** Assume "Pro Se" is stamped across your brief. Overcome it with clarity and discipline.

Why This Works

- Trial judges may dismiss you, but appellate courts read the paper. Precision exposes bias.
- The stigma cannot be erased, but it can be reversed: what begins as contempt becomes your proof of systemic misconduct.
- Over time, disciplined filings shift perception from "nuisance" to "dangerous opponent."

Rule of War:

Pro Se is meant to be your scarlet letter. Wear it as armor. Reflect every sneer back into the record until the stigma becomes their confession.

"There are, for example, so many kinds of voices in this world, and none is without its own signification." (1 Cor. 14:10)

Chapter 56 – Doctrine of Malpractice Leverage

"He that diggeth a pit, shall fall into it: and he that rolleth a stone, it shall return to him." (Prov. 26:27)

BLUF (Bottom Line Up Front)

Opposing counsel's greatest fear is not losing to you—it is being sanctioned, disciplined, or sued because of you. Lawyers practice under the constant shadow of malpractice exposure and bar complaints. The Doctrine of Malpractice Leverage means you deliberately frame your filings, objections, and record-building to turn every mistake they make into a professional liability risk.

The Doctrine

Malpractice Leverage turns opposing counsel's own professional obligations into pressure points—quietly, procedurally, and with precision.

Lawyers fear:

- disciplinary referrals,
- sanctions motions,

- malpractice claims,
- ODC complaints,
- insurer notification,
- reputational damage inside their firm.

Unlike judges, attorneys cannot ignore these pressures. Unlike clerks, they are personally exposed. Unlike the system, their livelihood is on the line.

This doctrine does not require threats, drama, or emotion—only verification, documentation, and disciplined use of the rules they already fear. Every procedural defect you preserve becomes a potential liability event for them.

You do not attack the lawyer directly.
You build the record so that **the record attacks them**.

Malpractice Leverage synergizes with:

- Procedural Mirror,
- Verification Doctrine,
- Sanctions Doctrine,
- Counter-Manipulation,
- AI-Assisted Briefcraft.

Your goal is not punishment—it is advantage. When their license is at stake, they become cautious, sloppy, divided, and afraid. And fear is leverage.

Rules of the Doctrine

Rule 1: Document Everything They Do.

Every missed service, misstatement, backdated filing, or procedural defect becomes an exhibit. Lawyers fear the record.

Rule 2: Frame Misconduct in Their Language.

Use "procedural defect," "variance," "irregularity," "noncompliance with Rule X."
Never "fraud." They know which words trigger discipline.

Rule 3: File Sanctions Motions With Judicial Notices.

- Motion = compels action.
- Judicial Notice = preserves the misconduct for appeal, ODC, or malpractice claim.

Dual fronts create unavoidable pressure.

Rule 4: Target the Professional, Not the Personality.

Every argument has two layers:

- Why the issue is legally yours, and
- Why opposing counsel's conduct violates Pa.R.C.P. 1023.1 or Pa.R.P.C. 3.3.

Lawyers read ethics rules like soldiers read landmines.

Rule 5: Escalate Quietly and Relentlessly.

You never threaten. You document.
If misconduct persists, escalate to ODC, bar referrals, or

federal §1983 filings for obstruction.
Nothing terrifies a lawyer more than quiet precision.

Tactical Applications

- **Missed Service:**
  Judicial Notice of Lack of Service + Motion for Sanctions (Pa.R.C.P. 440).
- **False Statement:**
  Judicial Notice of Misrepresentation + Pa.R.P.C. 3.3(c).
- **Backdating:**
  Judicial Notice of Metadata Variance + Motion to Strike.
- **Conflict of Interest:**
  Judicial Notice of Non-Waivable Conflict + Motion to Disqualify.

Each step transforms opposing counsel from "wrong" into "professionally reckless."

Each step strengthens your record *and* increases their career risk.

Why This Works

- Judges may ignore you—**lawyers cannot ignore bar exposure**.

Reporting obligations, assessor notifications, and client relations force attention.

- It splits the enemy.

Clients lose trust. Firms force settlement. Insurers intervene.

- It changes who they think you are.

Not “Pro Se nuisance”—but a procedural threat capable of triggering discipline.

- It exploits a structural vulnerability.

The bar protects its own—but not when they endanger the bar.

Rule of War:

The bar protects its own—until you make their misconduct a liability they cannot ignore. The Doctrine of Malpractice Leverage ensures every slip by opposing counsel becomes a sword hanging over their career.

“For in what things a man shall sin, in those also shall he be punished.” (Wisdom 11:17—note: deuterocanonical, Catholic Old Testament)

Chapter 57 – Doctrine of False Reforms

"This people honoureth me with their lips: but their heart is far from me." (Isaiah 29:13)

BLUF (Bottom Line Up Front):

The system will pretend to help you. Courts point to "Pro Se reforms"—help desks, self–help booklets, clerks, kiosks, even special offices—as proof that you are treated fairly. The numbers prove otherwise. The Doctrine of False Reforms means you recognize these programs as placebo, designed to protect the system's legitimacy, not to change outcomes.

The Doctrine

Pro Se reforms are not designed to improve outcomes—they are designed to preserve legitimacy.

Help desks, kiosks, clerks, and booklets make courts appear fair while leaving every structural disadvantage intact. The label "Pro Se" still signals incompetence. Bias still shapes the judge's posture. Procedural discretion still shields opposing counsel. And the win-rate data proves that none of these reforms change anything.

False Reforms operate as institutional theater: a performance of assistance without the substance of relief. They soothe the public, protect the courts, and give judges rhetorical cover—"you had resources."

But they do not alter access to the record, enforcement of rules, or judicial discretion.

Doctrine exists because reforms do not work.
Only disciplined filings, verified notices, Visual Law, metadata preservation, and Exhaustion change outcomes.

False Reforms remind you of one principle:
the system will pretend to help you, but only doctrine will save you.

The Illusion of Reform

- **Federal data:** Pro se plaintiffs win **3–4% of cases**, defendants lose **80–90%**.
- **Chicago Law Review study:** Courts that implemented reforms (help desks, Pro Se clerks, CM/ECF access, handbooks) had **no better outcomes** than courts that did nothing.
- **Cornell study:** Even when courts expand Pro Se resources, litigants still fail at basic thresholds (motions to dismiss, evidentiary burdens) because reforms do not alter judicial bias or systemic discretion.
- Judges and clerks *say* reforms are effective, but empirical analysis proves they are not.

Translation: These reforms exist to reassure the public, not to help you win.

Why Reforms Fail

1. **They Do not Change Bias.** Judges still treat "Pro Se" as a negative signal. A kiosk form does not erase prejudice.
2. **They Do not Enforce Rules.** Opposing counsel can still lie, mis–serve, or backdate. No "help center" stops that.
3. **They Do not Compel Rulings.** A handbook cannot force a judge to schedule your motion or stop docket suppression.
4. **They Do not Alter Outcomes.** All studies show win rates remain flat, no matter how many reforms are implemented.

Rules of the Doctrine

Rule 1: Trust Nothing Labeled "Pro Se Reform." Assume every handbook or help desk is a placebo.

Rule 2: Treat Reforms as Cover, Not Substance. When a judge says "we have resources for Pro Se litigants," you know they are shielding bias.

Rule 3: Never Depend on Their Tools. File your own verified motions, notices, and proposed orders. Do not rely on court–prepared forms alone.

Rule 4: Use Their Reforms Against Them. If they claim reforms exist, cite the empirical evidence: outcomes do not improve despite reforms. This undercuts their legitimacy.

Rule 5: Anchor in Exhaustion. Reforms are distractions. Exhaustion doctrine—pounding the trial court until silence becomes confession—is the only real reform.

Tactical Applications

- **Judge cites help desks:** Respond: "Respectfully, empirical data shows Pro Se reforms do not alter outcomes; case law and verified filings remain the only path to relief."
- **Court points to Pro Se clerks:** File Judicial Notice documenting unrebutted statistics (3–4% win rate despite reforms).
- **Opposing counsel mocks you for using forms:** Counter with verifications, exhibits, and citations—things reforms never teach.

Why This Works

- **You pierce the illusion.** Courts use reforms to argue Pro Se get a "fair shot." Documenting their ineffectiveness makes appellate courts confront systemic bias.

- **You deny them legitimacy.** Every time they say "you had help," you counter with the data showing it was meaningless.
- **You show why doctrine is essential.** Without doctrines like Exhaustion and Mirror, the best a Pro Se help desk can offer is a cleanly typed loss.

Rule of War:

Reforms are theater. The Doctrine of False Reforms reminds you never to be lulled by pamphlets or kiosks. Only relentless, verified filings—not placebo programs—alter the record.

"Having an appearance indeed of godliness, but denying the power thereof." (2 Tim. 3:5)

Part VI: Advanced Doctrines

Chapter 58 – Doctrine of Parallel Venue Fraud

"Woe to them that devise iniquity, and work evil in their beds: in the morning light they execute it, because their hand is against God." (Micah 2:1)

BLUF (Bottom Line Up Front)

When your opponent cannot win in the primary court, they will try to open a second battlefield behind your back.
Parallel venue fraud is the deliberate use of multiple counties or jurisdictions—often with defective service or stale judgments—to create confusion, multiply pressure, and end-run your defenses.
The doctrine is simple: link the venues, expose the duplication, strike the weaker judgment, and force all actions into a single, lawful forum.
You do not let them fight you twice. You collapse the second venue and make it their confession.

The Doctrine:
When your opponent cannot win in one courtroom, they open a second front in another. Parallel venue fraud is the practice of pursuing **duplicative enforcement or**

judgments in different counties to multiply pressure, confuse the record, and drain your resources.

Parallel venue fraud succeeds because courts operate in silos; one venue does not know what the other is doing unless you force the linkage.

Venue multiplication is not a mistake—it is a strategy, and courts will not connect the dots unless you force them.

Rules of the Doctrine

Rule 1: Always assume a second venue exists until you prove it does not.

Opponents who cannot win on the merits often file in another county or jurisdiction, hoping you never look. Your first task in any litigation is docket reconnaissance in every adjoining county.

Rule 2: Link the venues immediately—do not let the courts operate in isolation.

A Judicial Notice of Related Action collapses the artificial separation and forces both courts to acknowledge the duplicative proceeding. Fragmentation is their weapon; linkage is yours.

Rule 3: Attack service first—defective service is the weak seam in every parallel action.

Venue fraud almost always depends on:

- stale service,
- improper service,

- no service, or
- fabricated service.

A Petition to Strike for defective service destroys the secondary judgment at its root.

Rule 4: Use jurisdiction as the blade.

Two courts cannot simultaneously exercise authority over the same claim, judgment, or party without statutory authorization. Show the conflict, cite the statute, and you force one venue to yield.

Rule 5: Freeze the secondary battlefield with a Stay of Enforcement.

The moment duplication is discovered, move for a stay. A frozen venue is a defeated venue. Stays protect the record, prevent asset seizure, and expose the opponent's intent.

Rule 6: Make duplication their confession.

Parallel filings, inconsistent affidavits, competing writs, and mismatched service returns become Visual Law evidence of bad faith. Do not accuse. Display the structure. Let the record speak.

Rule 7: Collapse the weaker judgment to strengthen the stronger appeal.

Striking the parallel venue's defective judgment forces the primary court to confront the manipulation. Appellate courts understand one truth clearly: honest litigants do not forum–shop in the dark.

Tactical Applications

- Always check other county dockets.
- File **Judicial Notice of Related Action** in your main case to expose the duplication.
- File a **Petition to Strike Judgment** in the parallel venue if service was defective (almost always true).
- Demand a **Stay of Enforcement** until the jurisdictional issue is resolved.

Case Study (*William H. Clinger Corporation (WHC) v. Michael V. Clinger*, Delaware County, PA, 2020)

In *WHC v. Clinger (2020)*, Plaintiff's counsel filed a **Praecipe for Writ of Revival** in Chester County on a 2021 judgment never properly served. At the same time, they sought enforcement in Delaware County. By filing Judicial Notice in Delco and a Petition to Strike in Chester, Defendant cut off the double–track maneuver.

Rule of War:

Expose the second battlefield before they ambush you. Link the cases, strike the weaker judgment, and show the court the fraud of fighting in two places at once.

"A double minded man is inconstant in all his ways." (James 1:8)

Chapter 59 – Doctrine of the Digital Fingerprint

"For behold thou hast loved truth: the uncertain and hidden things of thy wisdom thou hast made manifest to me." (Ps. 50:8)

BLUF (Bottom Line Up Front)

Courts can falsify dates, alter transcripts, and bury filings—but they cannot erase the machine's memory.
Every PDF, order, transcript, and docket entry carries hidden metadata that records its true creation time, author, and modification history.
The Digital Fingerprint Doctrine turns that metadata into a weapon: exposing backdating, suppression, and clerical fraud with mechanical certainty.
When the written order lies, the metadata convicts—because the machine never conspires.

The Doctrine:

Digital evidence does not bend to judicial bias. Every PDF, transcript, and docket entry contains an invisible trail—

creation timestamps, author IDs, modification logs, file hashes—that exposes what the court hoped you would never see. Judges can misstate dates; clerks can suppress filings; transcripts can be curated and edited. But metadata cannot be persuaded, intimidated, or falsified without leaving a second layer of metadata proving the falsification.

The Digital Fingerprint Doctrine shifts the battleground from narrative to machine truth. You no longer argue about when an order was created—you prove it. You no longer plead that a filing was suppressed—you show the timestamp. You no longer accuse the court of altering transcripts—you present the audio hash mismatch.

Metadata converts speculation into evidence and judicial misconduct into mechanical fact. The machine testifies where humans lie.

Rules of the Doctrine

Rule 1: Always extract metadata—never trust docket dates.

The docket stamp is theater. The creation timestamp is truth.

Rule 2: Compare creation date, modification date, and docket date every time.

If they differ, you have structural proof of backdating or suppression.

Rule 3: Anchor metadata in Visual Law.

Use tables showing:

- Docket date
- PDF creation timestamp
- Difference (in hours/days)

This exposes manipulation without one emotional word.

Rule 4: Preserve the metadata immediately.

Save the PDF locally, screenshot the properties panel, and verify with a Judicial Notice.

Rule 5: Use Judicial Notice to convert metadata into evidence.

You do not accuse; you store the mechanical truth in the record.

Rule 6: Pair metadata with audio hashes, email timestamps, and service logs.

When all digital signals align, judicial lies collapse.

Rule 7: Treat metadata as the final witness.

It does not forget, and it does not conspire with the court.

Tactical Applications

- **Backdated Orders:**

Extract metadata → screenshot → Judicial Notice → Motion to Strike for irregularity.

- **Suppressed Filings:**

Compare your service timestamp to the docket entry timestamp → show gap → file Judicial Notice of Docket Suppression.

- **Transcript Manipulation:**

Compare audio file hash and timestamp to transcript PDF timestamp → file Judicial Notice of Transcript Variance.

- **Curated Opinions Uploaded Late:**

Show docket entry date vs. creation date → Visual Law table → appeal hook.

- **Conflicting Judgments in Parallel Venue Fraud:**

Use metadata to prove which judgment was created first—and which was manufactured later to support forum shopping.

Case Study:

In *WHC v. Clinger (2020)*, a Judge issued an order **back dated to July 29**, but metadata showed it was created **July 30 at 12:29 p.m.**—after Defendant's midnight filing. This exposed docket tampering and fraud on the court.

Rule of War:

The pen may lie, but the machine never does. Metadata is the fingerprint of fraud—use it to prove what they thought could never be proven.

"There is nothing covered, that shall not be revealed: nor hidden, that shall not be known." (Luke 12:2)

Chapter 60 – Doctrine of Privilege Weaponization

"Woe to you that call evil good, and good evil: that put darkness for light, and light for darkness." (Isaiah 5:20)

BLUF (Bottom Line Up Front)

When opposing counsel waves a privileged document in court, they are not showing strength—they are confessing desperation.
Weaponizing privilege is a violation of ethics, evidence rules, and due process, and it instantly shifts the burden onto them.
The moment they breach privilege, you gain the advantage: you move to strike, demand return and destruction, invoke Pa.R.E. 502 and Pa.R.C.P. 4003.3, and seek sanctions for fraud upon the court.

Their misconduct becomes your weapon—because privilege, once violated, turns every step they take into liability.

The Doctrine:

Privilege exists to protect the most sacred space in law: the confidential communication between client and counsel. When opposing counsel weaponizes privileged material—by obtaining it improperly, misusing it in court, or "accidentally" attaching it to a filing—they are not attacking you; they are confessing malpractice.

Privilege breaches are not legal arguments.
They are professional detonations.

The Doctrine of Privilege Weaponization reframes their misconduct as your opportunity. You do not argue emotion. You do not debate relevance. You enforce the structural law:

> **Pa.R.E. 502:** Privilege is not waived by inadvertent or improper disclosure absent intentional relinquishment under governing law.
> **Pa.R.C.P. 4003.3:** attorney work-product cannot be invaded except under extraordinary necessity.
> **Pa.R.P.C. 4.4(b):** lawyers must stop reading privileged materials and notify the holder immediately.
> **Pa.R.P.C. 3.3:** they may not knowingly offer prohibited evidence.

A breach of privilege automatically opens multiple battlefields:

- motion practice,
- sanctions exposure,
- disciplinary referral,
- malpractice liability,
- appellate due-process arguments.

You do not attack the lawyer.
You let their breach attack them.

Privilege, once violated, turns every step they take into liability—because the law protects privilege far more strongly than it protects judges or lawyers.

Courts treat privilege violations as structural error—prejudice is presumed, and reversal is the default remedy.

Rules of the Doctrine

Rule 1: Treat every privilege breach as a structural violation, not an argument.

Privilege is absolute unless expressly waived. Theft, misservice, or misuse do not waive it.

Rule 2: Strike immediately and without debate.

Move to strike the privileged material and all references to it in any pleading or testimony.

Rule 3: Demand return, destruction, and certification.

Pa.R.P.C. 4.4(b) requires opposing counsel to stop reviewing privileged material and notify you. Demand written proof.

Rule 4: Turn the breach into a sanctions engine.

Cite Pa.R.C.P. 1023.1, Pa.R.P.C. 3.3, and to request fees and discipline.

Rule 5: Invoke privilege law with surgical precision.

Pa.R.E. 502(d): inadvertent disclosure is NOT waiver.
Pa.R.E. 502(b): no waiver without intentional relinquishment.

Rule 6: Preserve the appellate issue immediately.

A privilege breach violates due process—you must file Judicial Notice documenting the breach and the attempted use.

Rule 7: Never let them reframe the issue.

They will try to argue "relevance," "context," or "fairness." Your answer is always the same:

Privilege destroys admissibility. Intent is irrelevant.

Tactical Applications

• They use a privileged email:
→ File Motion to Strike + Judicial Notice of Privilege Breach
→ Demand destruction + Pa.R.P.C. 4.4(b) compliance
→ Seek sanctions under Pa.R.C.P. 1023.1

• They attach your work product (drafts, notes, legal strategy):
→ Cite Pa.R.C.P. 4003.3
→ Argue substantial hardship test is unmet
→ Demand immediate sealing and protective order

• They wave a privileged communication in court:
→ Object instantly: "Privileged material—Move to Strike."
→ Request curative instruction or mistrial
→ File Judicial Notice within 24 hours

• **They claim "you waived privilege":**
→ Cite Pa.R.E. 502(b), 502(c)—waiver requires intent
→ Show no intentional relinquishment occurred
→ File metadata showing they obtained the document improperly

• **They use jailhouse letters, intercepted emails, or surveillance-acquired documents:**
→ Argue unlawful acquisition → request suppression
→ Move to sanction for attempting to introduce contraband privilege

Privilege breaches are the rare procedural moments where the Pro Se litigant has superior weapons—because the law takes privilege more seriously than anything else.

Appellate courts reverse more often for privilege violations than for nearly any other evidentiary error. Privilege is treated as **structural**—meaning prejudice is presumed.

Privilege belongs to the client alone; counsel cannot waive it for you, intentionally or otherwise.

Rule of War:

When they weaponize your privilege, they hand you the gun. Pick it up, aim it back, and fire with sanctions.

"For nothing is hidden that shall not be made manifest, nor secret that shall not be known and come to light."
— Luke 8:17

Chapter 61 – Doctrine of the Exit Ramp

"Stand in the ways, and see, and ask for the old paths, which is the good way, and walk ye in it: and you shall find refreshment for your souls." (Jer. 6:16)

BLUF (Bottom Line Up Front)

Judges avoid confrontation whenever possible. When a case becomes politically dangerous, procedurally messy, or fraught with misconduct, the court looks for a clean, lawful way to end the conflict without exposing itself.

The Exit Ramp Doctrine gives the judge that path: a narrow, verified request for declaratory relief that resolves the core issue without requiring the court to address the surrounding corruption.

You win by giving the judge the easiest lawful choice—a ruling so clean and limited that taking it becomes the path of least resistance.

The Doctrine

Exit Ramp Doctrine reframes the conflict from chaos to clarity. Instead of asking the court to referee misconduct, sanction attorneys, or unwind procedural fraud, you ask for a single, narrow declaration grounded in uncontested law. Judges choose the path of least resistance, and declaratory relief becomes the cleanest lawful way to end the case without touching the corruption you have documented for appeal.

Declaratory relief is strongest when paired with Judicial Notices documenting the surrounding misconduct—not to force the judge to address it, but to preserve it for appeal.

Rules of the Doctrine

Rule 1: Narrow the question until the answer becomes inevitable.

Declaratory relief must reduce the conflict to a yes/no legal determination.

Rule 2: Anchor the request in verified, uncontested documents.

Stock certificates, transfer instruments, bylaws, timestamps—judges prefer evidence that cannot be argued with.

Rule 3: Ask for clarity, not justice.

Judges avoid sanctioning lawyers or unraveling fraud; they welcome ruling on a clean legal question.

Rule 4: Separate the declaration from the consequences.

Let malpractice, sanctions, and disciplinary fallout occur downstream.

Rule 5: Build the offramp the judge wants, not the ruling you emotionally prefer.

The narrowest lawful remedy is usually the path the judge will choose.

Tactical Applications

- File a **Verified Petition for Declaratory Judgment** (42 Pa.C.S. §§ 7531–7541).
- Anchor it in **black–letter corporate law** (stock certificates, transfer instruments).
- Ask for nothing more than a **clear declaration of ownership or rights.**
- Let the fallout (sanctions, malpractice suits, disciplinary complaints) hit your opponent downstream.
- In federal court, the same strategy is executed under 28 U.S.C. § 2201 (Declaratory Judgment Act). The principle is identical: create the cleanest legal question and force the judge into the narrowest lawful ruling.
- The Exit Ramp shifts the risk burden entirely onto the opposing party—because the judge can grant declaratory relief without endorsing their misconduct.

- Declaratory relief avoids discovery, avoids evidentiary hearings, and avoids factfinding—three things judges are desperate to escape in contentious cases.

Rule of War:

Always build an exit ramp for the judge. They may not want to fight corruption head-on—but they will take the easy path of law if you pave it for them.

"Come to me, all you that labor, and are burdened, and I will refresh you." (Matt. 11:28)

Chapter 62 – Doctrine of Outcome Engineering

"Eye hath not seen, nor ear heard, neither hath it entered into the heart of man, what things God hath prepared for them that love him." (1 Cor. 2:9)

BLUF (Bottom Line Up Front):
Artificial intelligence can multiply speed, but only human imagination can bend trajectory. The disciplined litigant who uses AI as a *partner in invention*—not as a mechanical search bar—creates filings that shift outcomes rather than decorate the docket.

The Doctrine

Outcome Engineering is the doctrine that shifts litigation from reaction to creation.
Where lawyers look backward to precedent, the Pro Se strategist looks forward to outcome. Artificial intelligence accelerates research, but only human imagination can bend the trajectory of the case. PSLW teaches that every filing is not a recital of law—it is a designed move, an engineered prototype created to force a specific procedural or substantive outcome.

The system expects predictability: motions that look like motions, arguments that echo treatises, and filings that follow familiar scripts. Outcome Engineering breaks that expectation. It treats doctrine as principle, not limitation; AI as a co-architect, not a clerk; and each filing as an invention calibrated to close escape routes and compel lawful action.

You are not competing in elegance—you are engineering inevitability.
AI models possibilities; you choose the vector. AI refines structure; you supply the intent. Together, disciplined imagination and machine coherence create filings that courts have no template to resist.

Outcome Engineering reframes litigation as design:
a controlled fusion of creativity, verification, structure, and outcome.

Rules of the Doctrine

Rule 1: AI used for invention multiplies force; AI used for imitation multiplies noise.

The machine amplifies whatever you give it—creativity becomes leverage, replication becomes clutter.

Rule 2: Outcome is the only meaningful metric.

Form, elegance, and ritual are camouflage; filings are judged solely by whether they move the case toward relief.

Rule 3: Creativity without verification is chaos; verification without creativity is stagnation.

Imagination generates possibilities; verification anchors them in law. Both are required for strategic effect.

Rule 4: Humans imagine; machines refine.

You supply the vector, the machine supplies coherence. Together they reshape the procedural terrain.

Rule 5: Keep placing filings on the green until the record concedes the hole.

Every verified filing that forces the system to act—or refuses to act—inches the outcome toward inevitability.

The Tool of Invention

AI is not a typewriter with a search engine. It is a co-inventor waiting for command.

- The average lawyer uses AI to find cases.
- The warrior-strategist uses AI to *create law's next move.*

When you use AI to model outcomes, test arguments, and pre-empt objections, you are acting as an *inventor*, not a clerk.
You are designing each filing as a prototype in a laboratory of truth.

The Golf Analogy—Outcome Over Mechanics

Judges grade you by *where the ball lands*, not how pretty your swing looks.
A thousand words of proper form mean nothing if the motion misses the hole.
The Pro Se strategist aims for placement: every filing on the green, within striking distance of relief.
Mechanics are secondary. Results are record.

The Marine Analogy—Adapt and Overcome

In a field exercise, a Marine does not complain that the manual didn't cover this hill.
He studies terrain, improvises tools, and wins anyway.
Treat litigation the same way: doctrine gives you principles, not scripts.
Use imagination to bridge every gap doctrine cannot name.

How to Use AI as an Inventive Partner

1. **Ask Outcome Questions, Not Lookup Questions.**
   "Given these facts and statutes, what result becomes unavoidable?" —not "What cases say X?"

2. **Iterate Like an Engineer.**
   Feed your draft filings back into the machine for stress-tests: What objections remain? Where is the weak join?

3. **Preserve Human Command.**
   AI suggests; you decide. The moral vector stays human.

4. **Fuse Imagination and Discipline.**
   Unconventional formats, new combinations of rules, or novel analogies are lawful creativity, not chaos.
5. **End Each Cycle With Verification.**
   Every invention still obeys law—cite, verify, and lock it in the record.

Outcome Lens vs. Mechanics Lens

View	Question	Result
Mechanics Lens	"Did I follow every ritual?"	Safe but forgettable.
Outcome Lens	"Did this move the ball toward relief?"	Dangerous and decisive.

Stop counting strokes; watch the scoreboard.
Every verified filing that compels an honest act from the system is a win.

Rule of War:
Use the machine as your co-architect, not your clerk. File to invent, not to imitate. Win by imagination disciplined into law.

"Now unto Him who is able to do exceeding abundantly above all that we ask or think,
according to the power that worketh in us."
— Ephesians 3:20

Chapter 63 – Doctrine of the False Per Curiam

(Defeating Clerk-Issued Judicial Orders)

"The misleaders of my people have led them astray, and have disturbed the way of their paths." (Isaiah 3:12)

BLUF (Bottom Line Up Front)

A *Per Curiam* order is lawful only when it is **an act of the Court**.

Most appellate dismissals issued to Pro Se litigants are **not** acts of any judge—they are administrative denials fabricated by clerks who lack judicial authority.

A clerk cannot:

- dismiss a case,
- deny a motion,
- decide jurisdiction,
- close the record,
- or enter any dispositive judicial act.

A clerk-issued "Per Curiam" is not a judicial order.
It is **void ab initio**—legally nonexistent—and the case remains open for adjudication.

The Doctrine of the False Per Curiam teaches you how to expose this fraud, invalidate the clerk's action, restore judicial jurisdiction, and force a real judge to decide your case on the record you built.

You do not let clerks close your case.
You put the Court itself back on the hook.

The Doctrine

A false Per Curiam order is the appellate system's preferred weapon against Pro Se litigants.
The court avoids the work, avoids accountability, and avoids creating appealable rulings by letting clerks:

- mislabel filings,
- misroute motions,
- deny relief without panel review,
- dismiss appeals as "untimely,"
- or issue one-line "orders" that no judicial officer signed.

These are not mistakes—they are **structural suppressions** designed to keep your case off the books and out of the reporters.

The doctrine is simple:

A court speaks only through its judges.
A clerk has no judicial voice.
A clerk-issued order is not an order.

Your job is to:

1. **Expose the defect.**
2. **Force the Court to speak through a judge.**
3. **Preserve the invalid order as evidence of suppression.**

A False Per Curiam is not a setback —
it is a confession.

Rules of the Doctrine

Rule 1: A Per Curiam order without a judge's signature is void.

If no judicial officer signed it, the "order" has no legal force.
A clerk cannot adjudicate—only transmit.

Rule 2: Jurisdiction cannot terminate through administrative action.

Clerk-issued dismissals do not remove jurisdiction.
The case remains open in the eyes of the law.

Rule 3: A Court must act as a Court.

If the appellate panel did not review your motion, the "denial" is not judicial.
You file:

Judicial Notice of Non-Judicial Disposition of Judicial Act.

Rule 4: Force authentication.

Demand the Court identify the judicial officer who ordered the disposition:
"Name the judge or certify that no judge participated."
This corner checkmate never fails.

Rule 5: Misclassification is suppression.

Clerks routinely misclassify Rule 1701(b)(3) or 2572 motions as "reconsideration" to deny without panel review.
When that happens, you file:

Judicial Notice of Misclassification and Fraud on the Court.

Rule 6: A clerk cannot deny relief—only docket.

Any "denial" they issue is automatically void.
Treat it as non-action.
Trigger exhaustion.

Rule 7: A void order is not appealable—it is correctable.

You do not appeal a void act.
You demand a *judicial act* to replace it.
You force the Court to step onto the field.

Tactical Applications

1. When you receive an unsigned Per Curiam dismissal

File immediately:

Judicial Notice of Non-Judicial Order (Void Ab Initio) and a **Motion to Vacate Void Order**.

Grounds include:

- separation of powers (only judges may adjudicate),
- Pa.R.A.P. signature and authentication requirements,
- the ministerial nature of clerk and prothonotary duties,
- absence of judicial signature or panel identification,
- *Steel Co. v. Citizens for Better Environment* (jurisdiction cannot be presumed),
- fundamental due-process prohibition on deprivation of property or liberty without a judicial act.

A clerk-issued "order" is not a judicial act. It is legally nonexistent and cannot terminate jurisdiction.

---

2. When a clerk denies a petition, application, or motion

Respond in writing:

> *"Under Article V of the Pennsylvania Constitution, only a judicial officer may grant or deny relief. The Clerk's authority is ministerial only. A judicial ruling is required."*

Then file:

Judicial Notice of Ministerial/Non-Judicial Denial and

Application for Judicial Review by a Judge or Panel.

This forces the Court to confront the unauthorized disposition.

---

3. When a motion is misrouted to "administrative disposition"

Clerks often misroute dispositive filings to avoid judicial review.

File:

> **Judicial Notice of Misclassification of Judicial Act**
> and
> **Application for Panel Decision / Judicial Determination.**

State clearly:

"A dispositive motion cannot be resolved by administrative staff. A judicial officer must adjudicate or expressly decline jurisdiction."

---

4. When the appellate court "terminates jurisdiction" by clerk letter

Clerk letters have **no legal effect**. They are not judicial orders.

Treat them as non-action.

Then file:

Judicial Notice of Non-Judicial Attempt to Terminate Jurisdiction,

citing:

- signature requirements,
- ministerial limitations,
- due-process right to judicial determination,
- the continuing jurisdiction of the Court absent a judicial order.

Jurisdiction continues until a judge speaks.

---

5. When your filing is recharacterized (e.g., Rule 1701(b)(3) filing re-labeled as "reconsideration")

This is a common suppression tactic used to auto-deny filings without judicial review.

File:

Judicial Notice of Procedural Recharacterization
and
Motion to Correct Docket Classification.

Explain:

> *"The clerk lacks authority to recharacterize filings. Misclassification alters substantive rights and constitutes an unauthorized judicial act. A judge must classify, rule, or deny."*

This forces the Court to admit—or correct—the procedural manipulation.

Principle Underlying All Tactical Applications

A clerk or prothonotary may:

- timestamp,
- docket,
- transmit,
- archive.

A clerk or prothonotary may **not**:

- adjudicate,
- deny,
- dismiss,
- terminate jurisdiction,
- issue orders (including per curiams),
- recharacterize filings,
- decide appeals,
- create final judgments.

Any attempt to do so is void ab initio.

Every attempt must be met with:

1. **Judicial Notice** (to preserve the defect), and
2. **Motion to Vacate or Correct** (to compel a judge to act).

Rule of War

Clerks do not get to end your case.
Only a judge can speak for the Court —
and silence from the bench is not judgment.

Expose the False Per Curiam.
Force the Court to take judicial responsibility.
A case cannot die by clerk's pen.

Authority matters.
Command matters.
A clerk has neither.

"For with authority He commands even the unclean spirits, and they obey Him." (Mark 1:27)

Final Chapter 64—On Evil, Coherence, and the Restoration of Order

---

"You shall not pervert justice;
you shall not show partiality;
and you shall not take a bribe,
for a bribe blinds the eyes of the wise
and twists the words of the righteous.
Justice, and only justice, you shall pursue."
— Deuteronomy 16:19–20

BLUF (Bottom Line Up Front)

Evil, as injustice, is real.
But it is not all-powerful.

Evil does not survive truth.
It survives **incoherence**.

It flourishes where facts are fragmented, records are unfixed, decisions drift, and contradictions are allowed to coexist without consequence.

It collapses, **always**, when behavior is **observed**, **recorded**, and **forced into coherence**.

This is why the doctrines in this book work.

Doctrine of Coherence and Restoration

Rule 1—Evil Is Not a Thing; It Is a Condition

Evil is not always a crime.
It is not always a villain.
It is not always visible.

Evil is a **condition** that emerges when power is allowed to act without coherence.

Some are drawn to:

- authority without accountability,
- discretion without record,
- influence without consequence.

Others feel instinctive revulsion toward the same.

That is why people say, *"You know evil when you see it."*

They are right.

But knowing is not enough.
And outrage is useless.

Evil is not defeated by condemnation.
It is defeated by **constraint**.

Rule 2—Evil Requires Unresolved Contradiction

Evil requires only one thing to survive:

The tolerance of unresolved contradiction.

It requires:

- silence instead of rulings,
- delay instead of decisions,
- discretion instead of rules,
- narrative instead of record,
- power without attribution.

Where these conditions exist, injustice multiplies—even among people who would never call themselves corrupt.

Not because they are monsters.
But because **nothing forces coherence**.

Rule 3—What Is Unobserved Will Drift

Unobserved systems drift.

When no one is forced to:

- sign,
- rule,
- explain,
- or be compared,

precision disappears.

Rules soften.
Standards slide.

Exceptions become habits.
Habits become culture.

No one gathers to decide to be unjust.

They simply stop being exact.

This is how evil survives without ever announcing itself.

Rule 4—Coherence Is the Boundary Evil Cannot Cross

Evil can survive exposure.
It can survive denial.
It can survive outrage.
It can survive argument.

What it **cannot** survive is **coherence**.

Coherence means:

- facts align,
- timelines agree,
- records match actions,
- silence has meaning,
- contradictions are no longer tolerated.

Once coherence exists, evil has nowhere to hide.

Rule 5—Truth Can Be Argued; Coherence Cannot

Truth can be argued.
Truth can be relativized.
Truth can be mocked.
Truth can be voted down.

That is the lie of *"my truth"* and *"your truth."*

But coherence cannot be argued with.

You can debate what happened.
You cannot debate when **every independent fact tells the same story**.

You can debate intent.
You cannot debate when **documents, timestamps, actions, and silence all agree**.

This is why AI, as a partner and tool, matters in the practice of Pro Se Legal Warfare.

Not because it knows truth,
but because it reveals **coherence at scale**.

AI does not decide what is right.
It exposes what is **consistent**.

And evil cannot survive consistency.

Law as the Earthly Mirror of Order

Law, at its best, is not politics.
It is not preference.
It is not performance.

Law is the **earthly mirror of order**.

Rules, statutes, procedures, and records exist for one reason: to force human behavior into coherence.

When law is applied coherently, justice emerges naturally. When law is bent, blurred, or ignored, injustice follows just as naturally.

Courts fail not because law is weak—
but because coherence is abandoned.

Doctrine in Action: The Final Triad

The Triad of Restoration

Observation · Record · Coherence

1. **Observation**
   You watch without flinching.
   You do not look away.
   You do not accept silence as neutrality.

2. **Record**
   You document.
   You verify.
   You fix events in time so they cannot drift.

3. **Coherence**
   You align facts until contradiction collapses.
   You let law—not emotion—do the work.

This is not rebellion.
This is **restoration**.

Why One Person Matters

One disciplined person can do what outrage never will:

One can **force coherence**.

One does not let silence evaporate.
One does not let discretion float.
One does not let records dissolve.

One can turn noise and drift into data.

And because most systems are built on tolerated incoherence,
one coherent actor destabilizes the entire structure.

They were trained for darkness.
They were trained for informality.
They were trained for unobserved power.

They were not trained for you.

Why Many People Restore Sanity

Evil, and injustice, persists because coherence is rare.

When many people:

- observe,
- record,
- verify,
- and refuse to let contradictions survive,

the equilibrium breaks.

Not violently.
Not dramatically.
Not emotionally.

But permanently.

Systems that depend on incoherence cannot survive **sustained coherence**.

This is how injustice ends.
This is how sanity returns.

The Point of All This

This book was not written to make you angry.
It was written to make you **whole**.

Whole in thought.
Whole in purpose.
Whole in alignment with law, conscience, and truth.

A court should never be a place of helplessness.
It should be the place where coherence is revealed;
and where justice, inevitably, follows.

You are not here to imitate lawyers.
You are not here to please judges.
You are not here to perform.

You are here to **restore order where it has been abandoned**.

That is not rebellion.
That is stewardship.

Rule of War

Observe precisely.
Record relentlessly.
Force coherence.
Restoration follows.

— Final Law—Old Testament —

"Let justice roll down like waters,
and righteousness like an ever-flowing stream."
— Amos 5:24

Appendix A – Doctrine Rules Summary

Strategic Litigation Principles for Pro Se Warriors

Part I—Entering the Arena

1. Doctrine of the Cage Match

Doctrine: Court is combat, not ceremony.
Consequence: You win by strategy, not by believing the myth.

2. Doctrine of the Tilted Field

Doctrine: The system is biased at the start.
Consequence: Expect nothing; prepare for everything.

3. Doctrine of the Pro Se Advantage

Doctrine: Independence beats bureaucracy.
Consequence: You move faster than they can adapt.

Part II—The Rules of Engagement

4. Doctrine of Command, Not Prayer

Doctrine: Relief is demanded, not begged.
Consequence: Precision forces rulings; emotion invites dismissal.

5. Doctrine of the Adjudicator, Not the Court

Doctrine: Only judges judge; clerks do not rule.
Consequence: Identify the actor and attack jurisdiction at the source.

6. Doctrine of Jurisdictional Limits

Doctrine: Outside jurisdiction, nothing is lawful.
Consequence: Void acts collapse without resistance.

7. Doctrine of Love for the Law

Doctrine: Mastery creates advantage.
Consequence: Knowing law better than your opponent disarms them.

8. Doctrine of Mission Clarity

Doctrine: Define the objective before filing.
Consequence: Every motion becomes a step toward inevitability.

9. Doctrine of the Written Record

Doctrine: The record decides the case.
Consequence: What you do not file does not exist.

10. Doctrine of Appellate Vision

Doctrine: Write for the judge who isn't in the room.
Consequence: The appeal becomes unwinnable—for your opponent.

11. Doctrine of the Warrior's Posture

Doctrine: Calm precision is strength.
Consequence: Emotion confirms their stereotype; discipline destroys it.

12. Doctrine of First Blood

Doctrine: The first strike frames the war.
Consequence: Establish narrative, tone, and law before they do.

Part III—The Battle Plan

13. Doctrine of Measuring the Field

Doctrine: Map terrain before advancing.
Consequence: No ambush can surprise you.

14. Doctrine of Provocation

Doctrine: Force them to move first.
Consequence: Their reaction becomes your proof.

15. Doctrine of Precision Strikes

Doctrine: Short filings hit hardest.
Consequence: Courts follow clarity, not verbosity.

Part IV—Weapons of War (Core Doctrines)

16. Doctrine of Litigation as Signal Recovery

Doctrine: Filing transmits truth through noise.
Consequence: Structure reveals what bias tries to bury.

17. Doctrine of the Bellwether

Doctrine: Test the system with small filings.
Consequence: Their behavior reveals your strategy.

18. Doctrine of the Procedural Guillotine

Doctrine: One issue must end the case.
Consequence: A single error severs their entire position.

19. Doctrine of the Sur-Reply

Doctrine: Never allow the last word to stand.
Consequence: You close every escape hatch.

20. Doctrine of Silence

Doctrine: Silence is a weapon, not absence.
Consequence: They move into the trap you set.

21. Doctrine of Adverse Inference

Doctrine: Unrebutted fact becomes admitted fact.
Consequence: Their silence becomes your victory.

22. Doctrine of the Litigation Hold

Doctrine: Preservation begins immediately.
Consequence: Any destruction becomes their liability.

23. Doctrine of Spoliation

Doctrine: Destroyed evidence convicts the destroyer.
Consequence: Their misconduct becomes your proof.

24. Doctrine of the Audible Record

Doctrine: Audio is the true transcript.
Consequence: Curation collapses under comparison.

25. Doctrine Triad I—Velocity · Attrition · Minimalism

Doctrine: Speed, endurance, and simplicity overwhelm.
Consequence: The system cannot keep up.

26. Doctrine of Velocity

Doctrine: Act faster than they can process.
Consequence: You dictate tempo and overwhelm opposition.

27. Doctrine of Attrition

Doctrine: Persistence breaks resistance.
Consequence: They exhaust long before you do.

28. Doctrine of Procedural Minimalism

Doctrine: Least words, maximum force.
Consequence: Clarity compels rulings.

29. Doctrine of Veracity, Verification, and Sanctions

Doctrine: Verified filings are sworn evidence.
Consequence: Unrebutted verification boxes them in.

30. Doctrine of the Legal Incantation

Doctrine: Labels without evidence are not argument.
Consequence: Incantations collapse when unsupported by record or law.

31. Doctrine of Reputational Gravity

Doctrine: Earn weight through discipline.
Consequence: Judges treat you differently when the record demands it.

32. Doctrine of Tactical Saturation

Doctrine: Every filing must preserve, preempt, or position.
Consequence: They drown in obligation; you conserve strength.

33. Doctrine of Asymmetry Advantage

Doctrine: You are ungoverned; they are constrained.
Consequence: Their structure becomes your weakness to exploit.

34. Doctrine Triad II—Human Creativity · Strategic Imagination · Cognitive Alliance

Doctrine: Creativity breaks prediction; machine logic refines it.
Consequence: Imagination plus AI moves beyond their experience.

35. Doctrine of Human Creativity

Doctrine: Invent the move they cannot foresee.
Consequence: Pattern-bound systems collapse.

36. Doctrine of Strategic Imagination

Doctrine: Think in outcomes, not rituals.
Consequence: Every filing becomes inevitable.

37. Doctrine of Cognitive Alliance

Doctrine: Human intent + machine coherence = force.
Consequence: No institution can match the combination.

38. Doctrine of AI-Augmented Briefcraft

Doctrine: AI enforces coherence and detects contradiction.
Consequence: Filings become unassailable.

39. Doctrine of AI Counter-Lawfare

Doctrine: Opponents misusing AI expose themselves.
Consequence: Strike the fracture AI cannot hide.

40. Doctrine of the Suppression Trap

Doctrine: When they hide your filing, it becomes evidence.
Consequence: Silence turns into their confession.

Part V—Procedural Counter-Doctrines

41. Doctrine of Filing as a Matter of Right

Doctrine: The right to file cannot be taken.
Consequence: Any obstruction becomes a constitutional violation.

42. Doctrine of Watching the Docket

Doctrine: Docket timing is weaponized.
Consequence: Vigilance defeats ambush.

43. Doctrine of Motions vs. Judicial Notices

Doctrine: Motions compel; notices preserve.
Consequence: Filing both closes every exit.

44. Doctrine of Praecipes, Motions, and Judicial Notices

Doctrine: Each tool commands a different actor.
Consequence: You control judge, clerk, and record simultaneously.

45. Doctrine Triad III—Footnotes · Visual Law · Exhibits

Doctrine: Footnotes teach, tables compel, exhibits prove.
Consequence: You shape what the court sees and believes.

46. Doctrine of Footnotes as Weapons

Doctrine: Authority lives below the line.
Consequence: Footnotes win arguments judges never acknowledge.

47. Doctrine of Visual Law

Doctrine: If they cannot see it, it does not exist.
Consequence: Tables force rulings they cannot avoid.

48. Doctrine of Exhibits

Doctrine: Curate, excerpt, anchor.
Consequence: A perfect exhibit decides the issue.

49. Doctrine of Docket Integrity

Doctrine: Metadata defeats manipulation.
Consequence: Irregularities become irrefutable.

50. Doctrine of Counter-Manipulation

Doctrine: Every defect is ammunition.
Consequence: Their tricks build your appeal.

51. Doctrine of Procedural Mirror

Doctrine: Reflect manipulation into the record.
Consequence: Their conduct convicts them.

52. Doctrine of Exhaustion

Doctrine: Pound the trial court until nothing is unpreserved.
Consequence: Appeal becomes inevitable victory.

53. Doctrine of Appellate Exhaustion

Doctrine: Appeals are won below.
Consequence: Waiver dies in a fully preserved record.

54. Doctrine of How Judges and Lawyers See the Pro Se Litigant

Doctrine: Know their bias.
Consequence: Weaponize it into predictable mistakes.

55. Doctrine of the Signaling Effect

Doctrine: "Pro Se" is a stigma—flip the signal.
Consequence: Discipline turns contempt into evidence.

56. Doctrine of Malpractice Leverage

Doctrine: Lawyers fear sanctions more than loss.
Consequence: Their mistakes become your blades.

57. Doctrine of False Reforms

Doctrine: Pro Se reforms are theatre, not remedy.
Consequence: Only doctrine—not pamphlets—changes outcomes.

Part VI—Advanced Doctrines

58. Doctrine of Parallel Venue Fraud

Doctrine: Expose duplicative venues and collapse the weaker.
Consequence: Opponents cannot fight you twice.

59. Doctrine of the Digital Fingerprint

Doctrine: Metadata reveals manipulation.
Consequence: Backdating becomes self-proving fraud.

60. Doctrine of Privilege Weaponization

Doctrine: Privilege cannot be used as a sword.
Consequence: Their breach becomes your sanction engine.

61. Doctrine of the Exit Ramp

Doctrine: Give the judge a clean, narrow way out.
Consequence: Declaratory relief becomes the path of least resistance.

62. Doctrine of Outcome Engineering

Doctrine: Invent the move they cannot anticipate.
Consequence: AI refines what imagination creates.

63. Doctrine of the False Per Curiam

Doctrine: Unsigned orders are not orders.
Consequence: Clerks cannot terminate jurisdiction.

64. Final Doctrine of Coherence Restoration

Doctrine: Justice emerges from coherence; injustice persists through contradiction.
Consequence: When the record is aligned, discretion collapses and lawful outcomes follow.

Appendix B – Rules of War

"For the weapons of our warfare are not carnal, but mighty to God unto the pulling down of fortifications."
(2 Cor. 10:4)

Doctrine	**Summary**	**Rule of War**
Chapter 1 – Welcome to the Cage Match	Court is a Cage Match	Enter the cage knowing no one is coming to save you.
Chapter 2 – The Playing Field Is Tilted	Tilted Field	Accept the tilt and weaponize its angles.
Chapter 3 – The Pro Se Advantage	Pro Se Advantage	Your freedom is their weakness—move where they cannot.
Chapter 4 – Doctrine of Command, Not Prayer	Command vs Prayer	Pray to God. Command the court. Never invert the order.

Doctrine	Summary	Rule of War
Chapter 5 – Doctrine of the Adjudicator, Not the Court	Judge vs Court	Bind the judge to the record, not yourself to the judge.
Chapter 6 – Doctrine of Jurisdictional Limits	Jurisdiction Limits	A judge outside jurisdiction is only a man in a robe.
Chapter 7 – Doctrine of Love for the Law	Love for the Law	Love the law enough to demand its obedience.
Chapter 8 – Doctrine of Mission Clarity	Mission Clarity	If you do not know what you seek, they will define it for you.
Chapter 9 – Doctrine of the Written Record	The Written Record	Speak for the transcript; it outlives everyone in the room.
Chapter 10 – Doctrine of Appellate Vision	Appellate Vision	Write today for the judge you will meet tomorrow.
Chapter 11 – Doctrine of the Warrior's Posture	Warrior's Posture	Posture shapes perception—stand as one who cannot be dismissed.

Doctrine	Summary	Rule of War
Chapter 12 – Doctrine of First Blood	First Blood	Win the opening movement and the battle follows.
Chapter 13 – Doctrine of Measuring the Field	Measure the Field	See the field as it is, not as you wish it were.
Chapter 14 – Doctrine of Provocation	Provocation	Their misconduct is your evidence—let them hand it to you.
Chapter 15 – Doctrine of Precision Strikes	Precision Strikes	Strike only where the law guarantees victory.
Chapter 16 – Doctrine of Litigation As Signal Recovery	Signal Recovery	Extract the signal and make the noise irrelevant.
Chapter 17 – Doctrine of the Bellwether	Bellwether	Anchor everything to the fact that controls the rest.

Doctrine	Summary	Rule of War
Chapter 18 – Doctrine of the Procedural Guillotine	Procedural Guillotine	Give the rule, build the record, set the deadline—and then step back. When silence meets structure, the blade falls on its own.
Chapter 19 – Doctrine of the Sur–Reply	Sur–Reply	Claim the last coherent word and deny them escape.
Chapter 20 – Doctrine of Silence	Silence	Silence is a blade—draw it with intention.
Chapter 21 – Doctrine of Adverse Inference	Adverse Inference	What they avoid speaks louder than what they say.
Chapter 22 – Doctrine of the Litigation Hold	Litigation Hold	Freeze the evidence early, and every destruction becomes your proof.
Chapter 23 – Doctrine of Spoliation	Spoliation	When they destroy evidence, they destroy themselves.

Doctrine	Summary	Rule of War
Chapter 24 – Doctrine of the Audible Record	Audible Record	Say it cleanly once; let the record echo forever.
Chapter 25 – Doctrine Triad I—Velocity · Attrition · Minimalism	Velocity–Attrition–Minimalism	Strike quickly, endure quietly, and speak sparingly.
Chapter 26 – Doctrine of Velocity	Velocity	Control tempo—move fast enough to unsettle, slow enough to aim.
Chapter 27 – Doctrine of Attrition	Attrition	Outlast them with discipline, not emotion.
Chapter 28 – Doctrine of Procedural Minimalism	Procedural Minimalism	One perfect filing defeats ten imperfect ones.
Chapter 29—Doctrine of Veracity, Verification, and Sanctions	Verification & Sanctions	A verified fact is iron—unrebutted iron is judgment.

Doctrine	Summary	Rule of War
Chapter 30 – Doctrine of the Legal Incantation	Legal Incantation	Incantations collapse when unsupported by record or law.
Chapter 31 – Doctrine of Reputational Gravity	Reputational Gravity	Build such integrity that even enemies must orbit it.
Chapter 32 – Doctrine of Tactical Saturation	Tactical Saturation	Surround your truth so thoroughly they cannot look away.
Chapter 33 – Doctrine of Asymmetry Advantage	Asymmetry Advantage	Be fluid while they are rigid; be unexpected while they repeat.
Chapter 34 – Doctrine Triad II—Human Creativity · Strategic Imagination · Cognitive Alliance	Triad II – Cognitive Doctrines	Invent, imagine, and ally with AI to multiply force.

Doctrine	Summary	Rule of War
Chapter 35 – Doctrine of Human Creativity	Human Creativity	Invent the move they lack the imagination to predict.
Chapter 36 – Doctrine of Strategic Imagination	Strategic Imagination	See the endgame before the system sees the board.
Chapter 37 – Doctrine of Cognitive Alliance	Cognitive Alliance	You imagine; the machine clarifies; together you overwhelm.
Chapter 38 – Doctrine of AI-Augmented Bricfcraft	AI Briefcraft	Command the machine to enforce coherence—and coherence will cnforcc truth.
Chapter 39 – Doctrine of AI Counter-Lawfare	AI Counter–Lawfare	Their misuse of AI reveals their cracks—strike there.
Chapter 40 – Doctrine of the Suppression Trap	Suppression Trap	Every silence they force becomes evidence you preserve.

Doctrine	Summary	Rule of War
Chapter 41 – Doctrine of Filing as a Matter of Right	Filing is a Right	You file because the law commands it—not because they permit it.
Chapter 42 – Doctrine of Watching the Docket	Watch the Docket	The docket is the war map—monitor every movement.
Chapter 43 – Doctrine of Motions vs. Judicial Notices	Motions vs Notices	Preserve with Notice; compel with Motion; win with both.
Chapter 44 – Doctrine of Praecipes, Motions, and Judicial Notices	PMN Doctrine	Command the clerk, command the judge, bind the court.
Chapter 45 – Doctrine Triad III—Footnotes · Visual Law · Exhibits	Triad III – Documentation Weapons	Footnotes shape law, visuals force clarity, exhibits lock reality.

Doctrine	Summary	Rule of War
Chapter 46 – Doctrine of Footnotes as Weapons	Footnotes as Weapons	Whisper truth in the footnotes and the court will hear you.
Chapter 47 – Doctrine of Visual Law	Visual Law	Make the truth visible at a glance—tables win what words cannot.
Chapter 48 – Doctrine of Exhibits	Exhibits	Curate, don't dump; one lethal exhibit beats a box of paper.
Chapter 49 – Doctrine of Docket Integrity	Docket Integrity	Reveal the manipulation and let the docket convict them.
Chapter 50 – Doctrine of Counter–Manipulation	Counter–Manipulation	Use their tactic against them until it becomes your weapon.
Chapter 51 – Doctrine of Procedural Mirror	Procedural Mirror	Reflect their misconduct into the record so the appellate court cannot look away.
Chapter 52 – Doctrine of Exhaustion	Exhaustion	Finish every step; leave them no place to hide.

Doctrine	Summary	Rule of War
Chapter 53 – Doctrine of Appellate Exhaustion	Appellate Exhaustion	Build the appeal inside the trial court—every filing a brick.
Chapter 54 – Doctrine of How Judges and Lawyers See the Pro Se Litigant	How They See You	Their contempt is your evidence—document it.
Chapter 55 – Doctrine of the Signaling Effect	Signaling Effect	Your discipline becomes your signal—broadcast it.
Chapter 56 – Doctrine of Malpractice Leverage	Malpractice Leverage	Their fear of the bar is leverage—apply it carefully.
Chapter 57 – Doctrine of False Reforms	False Reforms	Every reform hides a trap—find the trap first.
Chapter 58 – Doctrine of Parallel Venue Fraud	Parallel Venue Fraud	Collapse the weaker venue—fight one war, not two.

Doctrine	Summary	Rule of War
Chapter 59 – Doctrine of the Digital Fingerprint	Digital Fingerprint	The pen may lie; the metadata never does.
Chapter 60 – Doctrine of Privilege Weaponization	Privilege Weaponization	If they violate privilege, they hand you the blade—use it.
Chapter 61 – Doctrine of the Exit Ramp	Exit Ramp	Give the judge the clean path and watch them take it.
Chapter 62 – Doctrine of Outcome Engineering	Outcome Engineering	Do not follow the terrain—reshape it.
Chapter 63 – Doctrine of the False Per Curiam	False Per Curiam	A case cannot die by clerk's pen. Only a judge can speak for the Court.
Final Chapter 64 - On Evil, Coherence, and the Restoration of Order	Coherence Prevails and Restores	Force coherence. Let the system break itself against the record

Appendix C—Bibliography

I. Foundational U.S. Supreme Court Cases

Pillars of PSLW doctrine—jurisdiction, due process, pleading sufficiency, structural rights, judicial limits, and access to courts.

- ***Ashcroft v. Iqbal***, 556 U.S. 662 (2009)
- ***Bell Atlantic Corp. v. Twombly***, 550 U.S. 544 (2007)
- ***Bounds v. Smith***, 430 U.S. 817 (1977)
- ***Caperton v. A.T. Massey Coal Co.***, 556 U.S. 868 (2009)
- ***Chambers v. Baltimore & Ohio R.R. Co.***, 207 U.S. 142 (1907)
- ***Chambers v. NASCO, Inc.***, 501 U.S. 32 (1991)
- ***Ex parte McCardle***, 74 U.S. (7 Wall.) 506 (1869)
- ***Ex parte Siebold***, 100 U.S. 371 (1879)
- ***Gideon v. Wainwright***, 372 U.S. 335 (1963)
- ***Kalb v. Feuerstein***, 308 U.S. 433 (1940)
- ***Mathews v. Eldridge***, 424 U.S. 319 (1976)
- ***Norton v. Shelby County***, 118 U.S. 425 (1886)
- ***Steel Co. v. Citizens for a Better Environment***, 523 U.S. 83 (1998)
- ***Stump v. Sparkman***, 435 U.S. 349 (1978)
- ***West v. Atkins***, 487 U.S. 42 (1988)

II. Federal Courts of Appeals—Structural, Procedural, and Evidentiary Cases

A. Jurisdiction, Void Orders, Structural Defects

- ***In re Westinghouse Securities Litigation***, 90 F.3d 696 (3d Cir. 1996).
- ***United States v. Wade***, 388 U.S. 218 (1967). *(Applied in PSLW for timing/record integrity.)*

B. Spoliation, Evidentiary Sanctions, and Adverse Inference

- ***Nation-Wide Check Corp. v. Forest Hills Distribs., Inc.***, 718 F.2d 88 (3d Cir. 1983)
- ***Leon v. IDX Sys. Corp.***, 541 F.3d 903 (9th Cir. 2008)
- ***Schmid v. Milwaukee Elec. Tool Corp.***, 13 F.3d 76 (3d Cir. 1994)
- ***Zubulake v. UBS Warburg LLC***, 229 F.R.D. 422 (S.D.N.Y. 2004)

C. Right of Access, Open Courts, and Procedural Due Process

- ***McCray v. Maryland***, 456 F.2d 1 (4th Cir. 1972)
- ***Smith v. United States Dist. Court Clerks***, 435 F.2d 1266 (10th Cir. 1971)

III. Pennsylvania Supreme Court & Commonwealth Court Cases

Directly relevant to docket integrity, Pro Se rights, jurisdictional limits, and procedural constraints.

- ***Commonwealth v. Williams***, 330 A.2d 602 (Pa. 1975)
- ***Kovski v. Lycoming County***, 2019 Pa. Commw. LEXIS 34 (Pa. Commw. Ct. 2019)
- **Commonwealth v. McClelland**, 233 A.3d 717 (Pa. 2020)
- ***In re J.M.P.***, 378 A.2d 312 (Pa. 1977)
- ***McEvoy v. Quaker City Cab Co.***, 110 A.2d 405 (Pa. 1955)
- ***Bundy v. Dep't of Corr.***, 243 A.3d 19 (Pa. 2020)

IV. Federal Statutory & Rule Authorities

Core statutory and rule frameworks used throughout PSLW doctrines.

Federal Statutes

- **28 U.S.C. § 2201–2202**—Declaratory Judgment Act.
- **42 U.S.C. §§ 1983, 1985, 1986**—Civil rights, conspiracy, neglect to prevent.

Federal Rules of Civil Procedure (FRCP)

- **Rule 11**—sanctions.
- **Rule 37(e)**—spoliation of electronically stored information.

- **Rule 56**—unrebutted factual admissions.

Federal Rules of Appellate Procedure (FRAP)

- **Rule 4**—filing deadlines, jurisdictional timing.
- **Rule 10(c)**—reconstruction of missing/incomplete record.

Federal Rules of Evidence (FRE)

- **Rule 201**—judicial notice of indisputable facts.

V. Pennsylvania Statutory & Rule Authorities

Statutes

- **18 Pa.C.S. § 4904**—Verification / unsworn falsification.
- **42 Pa.C.S. §§ 7531–7541**—Declaratory Judgments Act.

Pennsylvania Rules of Civil Procedure (Pa.R.C.P.)

- **Rule 208.3(b)**—unopposed motions granted as of right.
- **Rule 212.1(e)**—pretrial statements.
- **Rule 1029(b)**—admissions by silence.
- **Rule 1035.3(d)**—unrebutted facts deemed admitted.
- **Rule 4011**—protective orders.

Pennsylvania Rules of Appellate Procedure (Pa.R.A.P.)

- **Rule 1701(b)(3)**—trial court authority after appeal filed.
- **Rule 1926**—correction/modification of appellate record.
- **Rule 2572(b)**—remand of record; striking/adjusting record.

Pennsylvania Rules of Professional Conduct (Pa.R.P.C.), including Rules 3.3 and 4.4.

VI. Pro Se Litigation Empirical Authorities

Foundational empirical research proving systemic disadvantage of Pro Se litigants.

- **American Immigration Council**, *Access to Counsel in Immigration Court* (2016).
- **Center for American Progress**, *A Right to Counsel is a Right to a Fighting Chance* (2019).
- **Federal Judicial Center**, *Just the Facts: Trends in Pro Se Civil Litigation (2000–2019).*
- **Federal Judicial Center**, *Unchanging Rates of Pro Se Litigation in Federal Court* (2015).
- **Harvard Undergraduate Law Review**, *Lawyerless Justice: Stagnation and the Collapse of Civil Rights Enforcement* (2020).
- **Legal Services Corporation**, *Justice Gap Report* (2017 & 2022).

- **Littman,** *Empirical Patterns in Pro Se Litigation in Federal District Courts, 98 U. Chi. L. Rev.* (2021).
- **National Center for State Courts**, *Knowledge and Information Services: Access to Justice* (2016).
- **NCSC,** *Judges in Lawyerless Courts: The Experience of Self-Represented Litigants* (2016).
- **Quintanilla & Steele,** *The Signaling Effect of Pro Se Status, 94 Ind. L.J.* (2020).

VII. Pro Se Practice Manuals & Judiciary Publications

Practical sources that courts themselves use—and expect you to use.

- *Pro Se Handbook – Approved Version*, U.S. District Court (2019).
- *Guide: How to Write a Complaint*, U.S. Courts Pro Se Guide (2019).
- *Pro Se Case Management for Non-Prisoner Litigation*, Federal Judicial Center (2011).

VIII. Additional Foundational Case Law for Advanced Doctrines

Used throughout PSLW for Procedural Mirror, Docket Integrity, Suppression Trap, False Per Curiam, and Jurisdictional doctrines.

- ***Ex parte Siebold***, 100 U.S. 371 (1879)
- ***McCray v. Maryland***, 456 F.2d 1 (4th Cir. 1972)
- ***Norton v. Shelby County***, 118 U.S. 425 (1886)
- ***Steel Co. v. Citizens for a Better Env't***, 523 U.S. 83 (1998)

Index

How to Use This Index

Entries are organized to guide rapid doctrinal reference:

- **Doctrine**: all PSLW doctrines appear as subentries.
- **Laws of Pro Se Legal Warfare**: the complete 24-Law framework.
- **Cases** and **Statutes and Rules**: controlling authorities grouped for quick access.
- Key concepts and tools are indexed alphabetically.
- **See** and **see also** references connect related doctrines and operational techniques.

Use this Index to locate the controlling rule, supporting authority, and applicable method with minimal search.

T

U

V

W

Z

Epilogue – The 24 Laws of Pro Se Legal Warfare

---

1. The Law of the Record

What is written is real; everything else is noise.

2. The Law of Binary Judgment

Force every issue into yes/no; corruption dies in the gray.

3. The Law of Procedural Gravity

A clean record pulls the court into the only lawful outcome.

4. The Law of Silence

Silence is pressure—applied, not surrendered.

5. The Law of Unrebutted Fact

What they do not rebut, they legally admit.

6. The Law of Verification

Sworn truth outweighs unsupported argument—always.

7. The Law of Asymmetric Force

Institutions move slowly because they must; you strike fast because you can.

8. The Law of Predictive Filing

Write for the judge who will decide, not the one who merely presides.

9. The Law of Jurisdictional Life and Death

When a judge leaves the law, the judge leaves the court.

10. The Law of Procedural Irreversibility

Once filed, truth enters a world they cannot erase.

11. The Law of Preservation

If it is not preserved, it never existed; if preserved, it cannot be denied.

12. The Law of the Procedural Mirror

Reflect their misconduct until the reflection becomes evidence.

13. The Law of Documentary Dominion

Control what the court sees, and you control what the court can rule.

14. The Law of Endurance

Courts break the undisciplined; discipline breaks the court.

15. The Law of Evidentiary Scarcity

One verified fact outweighs volumes of irrelevant paper.

16. The Law of Exposure

What you illuminate becomes yours; what they hide becomes theirs.

17. The Law of Docket Supremacy

The docket is the case; everything else is theater.

18. The Law of the Digital Fingerprint

The pen may lie; the metadata never does.

19. The Law of Procedural Ambush

Move before they expect it; they cannot block what they cannot foresee.

20. The Law of Strategic Saturation

Fill the record with purpose—nothing more, nothing less.

21. The Law of the Exit Ramp

Give the judge the cleanest lawful path, and they will take it.

22. The Law of Cognitive Alliance

Humans imagine; machines refine. Together they reshape the terrain.

23. The Law of Strategic Imagination

Invent the move they cannot foresee; refine it until it becomes inevitable.

24. The Law of Coherence

Coherence is truth; incoherence is self-indictment.

These are the laws. Now enter the arena

Let the record speak for you, and,

STAND ON YOUR BRIEFS.

— New Testament —

"Judge not according to the appearance, but judge just judgment."
— John 7:24

"Blessed are they that hunger and thirst after justice: for they shall have their fill."
— Matthew 5:6

"For there is nothing hid, that shall not be made manifest: nor secret, that shall not be known and come abroad."
— Luke 8:17

"Be ye doers of the word, and not hearers only, deceiving your own selves."
— James 1:22

"Let all things be done decently, and according to order."
— 1 Corinthians 14:40

"And let us not be weary in doing good: for in due time we shall reap, not failing."
— Galatians 6:9

"But the fruit of the Spirit is charity, joy, peace, patience, benignity, goodness, long-suffering, mildness, faith, modesty, continency, chastity: against such there is no law."
— Galatians 5:22–23

"For the word of God is living and effectual, and more piercing than any two-edged sword."
— Hebrews 4:12

"It is finished." (John 19:30)

www.ingramcontent.com/pod-product-compliance
Lightning Source LLC
La Vergne TN
LVHW051053210926
848486LV00002B/98